Past-into-Present Series

THE MONARCHY

L. F. Hobley

B. T. BATSFORD LTD   London

First published 1972

© L. F. Hobley 1972

Filmset by Keyspools Ltd, Golborne, Lancs.

Printed and bound in Great Britain by
The Anchor Press Ltd, Tiptree, Essex
for the Publishers
B. T. Batsford Ltd, 4 Fitzhardinge Street, London W1H 0AH

ISBN 0 7134 1776 5

Acknowledgments

The Author and Publishers would like to thank the following for the illustrations which appear in this book: the British Museum for figs 1, 8, 16, 19; British Tourist Authority for fig. 59; H. Felton for fig. 17; Giraudon for fig. 5; Imperial War Museum for fig. 53; IPS for fig. 61; the Mansell Collection for figs 7, 9, 12, 13, 20–24, 27–32, 34, 35, 37, 39–41, 46; Metropolitan Museum of Art, N.Y. for figs 2, 4; National Portrait Gallery for figs 14, 36; Paul Popper for figs 57, 58, 60; Public Records Office for fig. 18; Radio Times Hulton Picture Library for figs 3, 6, 10, 11, 25, 26, 38, 44, 45, 49–52, 54, 55; George Rainbird for fig. 48; Topical Press for fig. 47; Syndication International for fig. 62; Windsor Royal Library for fig. 15.
Thanks are also due to Weidenfeld Ltd and Hutchinson Ltd for permission to use quotations from the books detailed in the Further Reading list.

Contents

The Illustrations

Introduction

The best reason why monarchy is a strong government is that it is an intelligible government. The mass of mankind understand it, and they hardly anywhere in the world understand any other. WALTER BAGEHOT, 1826–77, *The English Constitution.*

> *Is it not passing brave to be a king,*
> *And ride in triumph through Persepolis?*
> CHRISTOPHER MARLOWE, *Tamberlane.*

> *What is a King? A man condemned to bear*
> *The public burthen of a nation's care.*
> MATTHEW PRIOR, *Solomon.*

> *All kings is mostly rapscallions.*
> MARK TWAIN, *The Adventures of Huckleberry Finn.*

'There will soon be only five kings left,' said King Farouk of Egypt to Lord Boyd Orr in Cairo in 1951, 'the kings of England, Diamonds, Hearts, Spades and Clubs.' Many kings had already been toppled from their thrones when King Farouk made this statement, and others have followed since, including Farouk himself, but the existence of a king or queen in Britain seems to be almost as unquestioned in the world at large as that of the kings and queens of the card pack.

The English people pride themselves upon the fact that Britain is a democracy, where all the people have the right to take part in the election of members of Parliament who rule on behalf of the people – and yet a monarch still reigns over the land. This may not appear very logical, but the British people have never worked out a logical system of government. Instead they have adapted their form of government to suit changing circumstances; so gradually through many centuries the powers of British monarchs have been curtailed, and their functions have changed. It may be said that now the British Queen reigns but she does not rule. The story of this change is a long and interesting one.

1 The Origins of Kingship and Early Kings of Britain

Priest-Kings

From very early times most human societies have adopted some form of kingship, not only for leadership but because many people feel a need to be ruled; they feel unequal to the task of making all the vital decisions about themselves and their relations with their neighbours: they want someone who can shoulder their responsibilities.

In the early history of many countries the leaders were as much priests as kings. They carried out the magic ceremonies which were thought to ensure good hunting, they supervised sacrifices to the Earth Goddess, which would bring them a bountiful harvest.

Sometimes the king himself was the sacrifice, giving himself for the future good of his people. In many places the king was believed to be descended from the tribal or national god.

In some situations the functions of the king were mainly limited to military leadership, while the priests gave it their moral and magical support. Here is the account from the book of Samuel, of how the Israelites adopted kingship after being ruled by prophets and priests:

1 Effigy of Horus. The Pharaohs of Egypt claimed to be descended from the god Horus, who was often represented by his symbol, the falcon

2 David anointed by Samuel. From a dish of Byzantine silver ware, made in the early seventh century

8

Then all the leaders of Israel gathered themselves together, and came to Samuel unto Ramah, and said unto him, 'Behold, thou art old, and thy sons walk not in thy ways: now make us a king to judge us like all the nations.' . . .

And Samuel said, 'This will be the manner of the king that shall reign over you: He will take your sons, and appoint them for himself, for his chariots, and to be his horsemen; and some shall run before his chariots. And he will set them to ear his ground, and to reap his harvest, and to make his instruments of war, and instruments of his chariots.

And he will take your daughters to be confectionaries, and to be cooks and to be bakers. And he will take your fields and your vineyards, and your olive-yards, even the best of them, and give them to his servants.

And ye shall cry out in that day because of your king which ye shall have chosen you.'

Nevertheless the people said, 'Nay; but we will have a king over us; that we also may be like all the nations; and that our king may judge us, and go out before us, and fight our battles.' . . .

Then Samuel took a vial of oil, and poured it upon his (Saul's) head . . . and said to all the people, 'See ye him whom the Lord hath chosen, that there is none like him among all the people?' And all the people shouted, and said, 'God save the king.'

The Celts

We know little about the organisation of the earliest inhabitants of Britain. One of the first kings of whom we have any knowledge was the Celtic Cymbeline. The Latin form of his name was Cunobelinus, and this was the name he had stamped upon his gold coins. He ruled part of south-eastern England just before the beginning of the Roman conquest in AD 43.

His son was the famous Caractacus, who led the Britons against the Romans at the battle of the River Medway. He was captured in AD 51, and taken to Rome, where his proud and fearless bearing gained him much better treatment than was usually the lot of captured kings.

The other famous ruler of the Britons was Queen Boadicea or Boudicca. She was deposed and ill-treated by the Romans, but her people rose in revolt. She led them against the Romans, and the Britons who were friendly with them, and slaughtered them in thousands. When the Romans began to gain the upper hand, she poisoned herself.

The withdrawal of the Romans left Britain without any overall government, but defence against the invading Angles, Saxons and Jutes was improvised by King Ambrosius, who organised a successful counter attack which halted the Anglo-Saxon advance for many years.

It was probably during this time that the legendary King Arthur lived, and stories of his kingship over the Knights of the Round Table had great influence much later upon the kings and knights of the Middle Ages.

9

3 The Funeral of Edward the Confessor, proceeding towards Westminster Abbey. From the Bayeux Tapestry

Anglo-Saxon England

The Anglo-Saxons settled in tribal areas which gradually increased in size until there were about seven kingdoms in southern Britain. At first the Saxon Kings were leaders of groups of free warriors, all of whom followed certain customs. The king was expected to see that all obeyed these, and he himself enjoyed little privilege, and lived much as all the others.

As the kingdoms increased in size, the kings became more divorced from their subjects. The king had to deal with new problems, and here he might claim that he was king by the grace of God, and free to exercise absolute power in the government of the people God had submitted to his care.

Kingship thus came to have a dual function: the monarch was guardian of the rights of his people, and so subject to laws and customs, but he was also God's regent, with the arbitrary powers of God. This dual nature of kingship lay at the root of many of the crises in government, until the problem was finally solved in quite recent times.

In the ninth century, Wessex became the most powerful of the Anglo-Saxon kingdoms, and Egbert, who ruled from 802 to 839 claimed to be the king of all England. Queen Elizabeth II is directly descended from Egbert and the Royal House of Wessex.

Succession to the throne in the early English kingdom was not strictly hereditary – it was limited to the royal family, but not necessarily to the eldest son of the reigning king (the system known as primogeniture). The Witan, or meeting of principal nobles, had the right to elect the next king from among the members of the royal family.

Alfred the Great

Alfred the Great provides a good example of the position of the king in Anglo-Saxon times. As a child he visited Rome, and he based his ideas of kingship upon

Christianity. When the Danes overran his kingdom of Wessex, he led the army in person, and having defeated Guthrum, the Danish king, he persuaded him to become a Christian.

He then organised the defences of the country: he built a network of fortified places or burghs, in which stores and soldiers were kept, and to which people in the country round could go for protection in case of attack. A navy was built with the aid of shipbuilders hired from abroad. The army, mainly of peasant levies, was reorganised so that there were always some men serving, and others working on the land and providing supplies.

Alfred believed that the duties of kingship were much wider than defence and protection. He codified the laws, and enforced them, had schools built, and encouraged both adults and children to learn to read. He himself wrote books and translated others. He started the Anglo-Saxon Chronicle, a yearly history of the country.

The Normans

The Norman kings greatly strengthened the royal power. They ruled through a King's or Great Council, composed of the most important barons and churchmen, which they normally called three times a year, but in most matters the king's word was law. The biggest threat to the king's power came from the great nobles.

Throughout western Europe the Feudal System had gradually been established. The great lords or barons received land from the king in exchange for military service. In many cases, however, the nobles were encroaching upon the power of the king, raising private armies and defying the royal authority.

William the Conqueror (1066–1087) was an exceedingly strong personality and he took very definite steps to keep the nobles firmly under his control. In granting land, he gave no very large areas to any one man, except on the borders of Wales and Scotland, but scattered their fiefs in fairly small pieces in different parts of the country. Each noble was therefore surrounded by many neighbours, who would no doubt watch him jealously for any sign that he was building up forces that might be used against the king. It would be almost impossible for any noble to gather his forces in sufficient strength to trouble the king without the fact being known.

Another, and more revolutionary step was the oath at Salisbury. It was the normal feudal custom for the smaller landowners to take an oath of fealty to their local overlord, so should the overlord rebel against the king, he could expect his followers to support him. At Salisbury, however, William compelled all land-owners to take an oath of fealty directly to him, so it would be very difficult for a noble to obtain the support of his followers against the king. 'On that day,' says Edward Freeman, 'England became for ever a kingdom, one and indivisible, which since that day no man has dreamed of parting asunder.'

Under the feudal system, when a man died, his eldest son inherited all his land. This was known as the system of primogeniture. The king was the greatest landowner of all – in fact William claimed that all the land was his. He leased most of it to his followers, but he retained many areas as royal domains.

It was expected that these royal lands would pass to the king's eldest son at his death, and it therefore became natural to think that the kingship itself would also pass to the eldest son. In other words, it was no longer thought that a king could be even partly elected – the crown was considered to be entirely hereditary by the eldest son, or failing that by the nearest heir.

One of the factors limiting the king's power was that of the Church. William the Conqueror had seized England with the approval of the Pope, but the Popes claimed that they were appointed by God to have spiritual power over all Christian monarchs, a higher power than the political power of kings. Ultimately, therefore, they claimed power over all Christian rulers.

Henry I, (1100–1135) however, wrote to the Pope, and stated that 'the dignities and customs of the realm of England shall not be diminished in my life-time. Even if I should subject myself to this humiliation, which may God forbid, my barons and the people of England would not permit it.'

Henry also strengthened the 'king's law' as compared with the baronial courts by his system of itinerant justices, who travelled round the country judging important cases.

The Church claimed that it was only after the king had been annointed and crowned by the archbishop, as Saul had been annointed by Samuel, that he could truly claim to be the legitimate ruler. Stephen (1135–1154) proclaimed himself 'by the grace of God, with the consent of the clergy and the people, elected King of England, consecrated by William, Archbishop of Canterbury and confirmed by Innocent the Pontiff.'

2 The Plantagenets

Custom, that unwritten law
By which the people keep even kings in awe
CHARLES DAVENANT (1656–1714) *Circe* II, iii.

The King and the Church

Henry II (1154–1189) was the first of a long line of fourteen Plantagenet kings. His father, Count Geoffrey of Anjou, wore a gay sprig of yellow broom flower, *planta genista* in his helmet, and so gained the nickname of Plantagenet. The Norman kings kept on good terms with the Pope, and chose archbishops who co-operated with them. It was generally agreed at that time that all clergy accused of crime should be tried in church courts and not in the king's court. Henry was determined to assert the power of the king over that of the Church. He styled himself 'King by the Grace of God' with no reference to Pope or archbishop. He decided to abolish the church courts and by appointing his friend, Thomas Becket as Archbishop of Canterbury, hoped to bring the clergy under the jurisdiction of the king's court. Becket, however, as soon as he was appointed, became a fanatical supporter of the Church point of view. After bitter words and the exile of Becket, the archbishop was murdered in his own cathedral. There was such an outcry that Henry had to give up all his efforts to abolish the church courts. For the next four centuries the church courts continued to operate independently of the king's courts, and the archbishop of Canterbury was sometimes ready to join with dissatisfied nobles in leading opposition to the king.

4 King Henry II and Queen Eleanor, carved in high relief. From the twelfth century church of Notre Dame du Bourg

In other spheres, however, Henry II greatly strengthened the power of the king, and restored order after the 'nineteen long winters' of Stephen's reign. He replaced corrupt local governors by his own trained men, and introduced an effective jury system. People then looked to the king and his appointees for justice and good rule.

King John: The King, Pope and Barons

The position of the king was affected in several ways during the reign of King John (1199–1216). The direct heir according to the principle of primogeniture was not John, but Prince Arthur, John's elder brother's son. The fact that John succeeded was evidence that there was still an element of the right of election. A sign of the close connection of the throne with landowning was that John was entitled King of England, not King of the English.

John quarrelled with the Pope. Here is an extract from Shakespeare's *King John*. The king replied to Cardinal Pandolph, the Pope's legate:

> What earthly name to interrogatories
> Can task the free breath of a sacred King?
> Thou canst not, cardinal, devise a name
> So slight, unworthy and ridiculous,
> To charge me to an answer, as the pope.
> Tell him this tale; and from the mouth of England
> Add thus much more, that no Italian priest
> Shall tithe or toll in our dominions;
> But as we, under heaven, are supreme head,
> So under Him that great supremacy,
> Where we do reign, we will alone uphold
> Without the assistance of a mortal hand:
> So tell the pope, all reverence set apart
> To him and his usurp'd authority. (Act III – Scene 1.)

But when things went badly with John, he agreed to accept the crown from the

6 Effigy of King John in Worcester Cathedral

Pope's Legate, and to continue to make payments to Rome. The English Monarchy could not yet claim that it was under no one save God. The fighting speech which Shakespeare puts into John's mouth represents the position in the late fourteenth century or even sixteenth century rather than the early thirteenth century.

Magna Carta

The most famous event of John's reign was the sealing of Magna Carta when Stephen Langton, Archbishop of Canterbury, led the barons in a protest against the way John was misgoverning the country. The Magna Carta was on the whole a backward-looking document, seeking to enforce upon the king the recognition of the customary rights and privileges which barons, church and freemen had gained in the past and the responsibility of the king to preserve them. It came

7 Constantine bestowing temporal authority upon the Pope, handing him the symbol of authority. From a twelfth century fresco

8 King John hunting stags. From the thirteenth century Cotton Manuscript

9 The Great Seal of King John

10 King Edward I in council with bishops and attendants. The scribes are made smaller to signify their unimportance

nearer than any other statute to making government a compact between a monarch who agreed to rule in accordance with law and custom and his subjects who therefore agreed to obey him. It suggested that the subject has a legal right to resist an unjust king. It came to be looked upon as a corner-stone of the Englishman's liberty, not so much because of what it said as because it stood for the right of the people of England to force concessions from an unjust king.

The King and the Beginning of Parliament

The right to force concessions from the king was put into practice during the reign of Henry III (1216–1272), when Simon de Montfort led the discontented barons against the king. To strengthen his party, he called to his support representatives of the communes, the chief citizens from the growing towns and the squires of the counties. This was the beginning of parliament as we know it and when Edward I became king, he followed de Montfort's example and called the Model Parliament of 1295.

At first the function of Parliament was to assist the king by providing him with information as to the state of the country, what revenue he could expect and the best way of raising it.

Edward I (1272–1307) was away upon a crusade when his father died. Within four days the barons had met and declared that Edward was king – they did not wait for his homecoming, or for a coronation, a ceremony which had previously been considered as essential before a man could be considered truly king. Hereditary right, and acceptance by the barons were now considered the only two necessary conditions. Edward II (1307–1327) succeeded his father without even being elected – to be the late king's eldest son was in itself sufficient.

11 King Edward I in Parliament, seated between King Alexander of Scotland and Prince Llewellyn of Wales

The fourteenth century was one of constitutional disputes and struggles. Hitherto, the king had been the source of justice: he had been responsible for the keeping of law, order and custom, and had himself sometimes made or amended the laws. Now Parliament was increasingly claiming a share in government, at first petitioning for new laws, which the king might accept and transform into statutes, or which he often refused or modified.

As Parliament's claims grew, so the kings tended to assert their royal powers and privileges, and to distinguish between these and their authority in and through Parliament. Any advantage gained by Parliament was regarded by the king as a limited privilege which was granted from the theoretically unlimited power of the sovereign through the use of the royal prerogative. From this idea, it later became possible for rebels to claim that although they were warring against the king's person, they were really defending the true royal power.

It was claimed that the king was under no one but God, and yet he was not above the law. As Parliament became increasingly responsible for law-making, there was therefore a continuing contradiction.

The Divine Right of Kings

Meanwhile in Europe the Pope had been increasing his claim that God had given him control over all kings. Against the Divine Right of the Pope, the kings of Europe maintained the Divine Right of Kings. In England, John Wycliffe wrote in *De Officis Regis* that the king is God's vicar in worldly things, while the priest is so in spiritual things. The king, he said, represented Christ's Godhead, but the priest represented Christ's manhood. The king was therefore superior to the Pope and his priests. This, he maintained, disposed of any claim by the Pope to exercise any control over the kings of England. The Statute of Praemunire of Richard II's reign (1367–1399) asserted that 'the crown of England hath been so free at all times that it hath been in no earthly subjugation in all things touching the royalty of the said crown.' If the crown, thought Richard, was not in any earthly subjection, it was no more subject to Parliament than to the Pope, and he claimed for himself Divine Right. He was the sole source of law and was not bound by custom. As king by God's grace and right of birth, he would not endure any interference with his freedom of action. He tampered with the Rolls of Parliament, he altered

12 The bones of John Wycliffe burned, forty-one years after his death, and cast into the river by the Bishop of Lincoln

and nullified statutes agreed by both houses of Parliament, and frequently absolved persons from obeying the law (used dispensing power). He packed Parliament with his own nominees, and bribed others, so that the Parliament of Shrewsbury, 1397–8, gave him power to arrange the order of business in Parliament, and so to ensure the granting of supplies before Parliament could present grievances. (The custom had been growing for Parliament not to grant supplies until the King had agreed to redress grievances.) He persuaded Parliament to delegate its power to a perpetual committee of eighteen. He thus was creating a series of Acts that would preserve the absolute right of the English crown. All future tenants, both barons and bishops were forced to swear to maintain these Acts before obtaining possession of their fiefs, and any attempt to repeal the Acts was declared to be high treason. Thus Richard II used Parliament to destroy Parliament's own liberties.

The Bishop of Exeter supported Richard's purpose in a sermon in which he claimed that it was God's will that the king alone ruled over all. A 'mixed Monarchy' (where the king shared power with others) led only to anarchy. The people must be obedient, declared the bishop, for the king was the source of all law, and judges were bound to maintain the rights of the crown. Richard maintained that nothing, not even his own deposition, could destroy his kingship, conferred by his royal birth and confirmed by the unction ceremony in the coronation.

When threatened by Bolingbroke's invasion, in Shakespeare's Tragedy of Richard II, he says –

> Revolt our subjects? that we cannot mend
> They break their faith to God as well as us . . .
> Not all the water in the rough rude sea
> Can wash the balm from an annointed king;
> The breath of worldly men cannot depose
> The deputy elected by the Lord:
> For every man that Bolingbroke hath press'd
> To lift shrewd steel against our golden crown,
> God for his Richard hath in heavenly pay
> A glorious angel: then, if angels fight
> Weak men must fall, for heaven still guards the right.

The Bishop of Carlisle spoke for a growing number of people who thought the subject owed complete obedience to the legitimate king –

> What subject can give sentence on his King?
> And who sits here that is not Richard's subject? . . .
> And shall the figure of God's majesty
> His captain, steward, deputy elect
> Anointed, crowned, planted many years,
> Be judg'd by subject and inferior breath?

13 Effigies of King Henry IV and his Queen, Joan of Navarre, on the tomb in Canterbury Cathedral

The deposition of Richard II in 1399 was a protest by the nobles against the despotic rule of a king who believed in his right to over-ride the laws and customs of the constitution. Their support for Henry of Bolingbroke as the new king was evidence that they had the right to elect the member of the royal family they thought the best fitted, for they passed over the nearest heir. Bolingbroke, however, did what he could to make his accession legitimate, by claiming that he was the nearest heir to Henry III, and although this was not generally believed, the fact that it was accepted is a sign that there was still widespread belief in the importance of legitimacy. With every change of ruler, claims were made that the new king had a legitimate right to the throne. Parliament often acted as a sort of supreme court which declared the law but did not claim the right to alter the succession. Henry IV was said to succeed 'through the right God had given him by conquest.' The statute declaring the succession of Richard III stated:

> . . . we consider that ye be the undoubted son and heir of Richard, late Duke of York, very inheritor of the said crown and dignitary royal, and as in right king

of England by way of inheritance . . . and by this our writing, choose you High and Mighty Prince, our King and Sovereign Lord. *To whom we know it appertaineth of inheritance so to be chosen.* . . . We pray and require your most noble grace according to this election of us the three estates of this land; as by your true inheritance you will accept and take upon you the said Crown and royal dignity with all things thereunto annexed and appertaining as to you of right belonging as well by inheritance, as by lawful election . . . (Speed's *History*, 724).

14 Portrait of King Henry VII

3 The Tudors

Kings climb to eminence
over men's graves.
A. DOBSON, Before Sedan.

Kings govern by means of popular assemblies
only when they cannot do without them.
C. J. FOX, Speech in the Commons, 1776.

Friend of my heart is it meet or wise
To warn the king of his enemies?
We know what Heaven or Hell may bring
But no man knoweth the mind of the king.
KIPLING, Barrack-room Ballads.

Henry VII

Henry VII (1485–1509) had very thin claims to the throne but he and his
supporters pronounced that the titles of all other claimants were void for some
reason – in descent through a woman, through a usurper, and so on. Henry's
father was Owen Tudor, a Welsh gentleman remotely descended from John of
Gaunt, fourth son of King Edward III. Henry who was Earl of Richmond, was
on the Lancastrian side of the Wars of the Roses, between the house of Lancaster
(the red rose) and York (the white rose) and had been exiled to France. By 1485
he was 'the nearest thing to royalty the Lancastrian party possessed'. When he
defeated and killed Richard III at the battle of Bosworth, he became King
Henry VII, the first Tudor sovereign. He strengthened his claim to the throne by
marrying Elizabeth of York, and so uniting the two rival houses.

By the end of the Wars of the Roses, the people of England were interested less
in a king's legitimacy than in his ability to rule strongly. The overwhelming desire

15 King Henry VIII in Parliament

16 The Coronation Oath of King Henry VIII, altered in his own hand at a later date when he declared himself Head of the Church and of England. The altered version reads (Henry's emendations in italics). 'The King shall swere that he shall kepe and mayntayene the *lawfull* right and the libertees of olde tyme graunted by the rightuous Cristen kinges of England *to the holy churche nott preiudyciall to hys jurydyction and dignite ryall* . . . And that he shall graunte to holde lawes and approved customes of the realme and *lawfull and nott preiudiciall to hys crowne or imperiall juris* (diction)'

of the English people during the Tudor period was for strong government, and an end to anarchy and civil war. Only a strong monarchy could do this, and writers and clergy all emphasised the importance of complete obedience to the sovereign. The statute granting the crown to Henry VII was a much more business-like statement of Parliament's power to decide the succession as it wished.

> Be it ordained established and enacted by authority of this present Parliament that the inheritance of the Crowns of the Realms of England and France with all the preeminence and dignity royal to the same appertaining . . . be, rest, remain, and abide in the most royal person of our now Sovereign Lord, King Henry the Seventh and the heirs of his body . . . and in none other (Statutes of the Realm, 11.499).

Henry VII extended the royal power by skilful government largely helped by the widespread desire for a king who could preserve law and order. He retained in royal hands a monopoly of the manufacture of gunpowder and artillery, forebade the keeping by the barons of armed and liveried retainers and set up the Court of the Star Chamber where even the mightiest noble could not overawe the king's judges. He fined offending nobles heavily and built up a large royal fortune.

Henry VIII (1509–1547)

Henry VIII still further strengthened the position of the king. He broke completely all links with the Pope and so ended the long struggle between the English kings and the Papacy. He became the Head of the English Protestant Church and thus ruled as the spiritual as well as the temporal head. Like Richard II, but more successfully, he used his Parliaments to increase the royal power. Most of the members of Parliament were glad to end making payments to Rome, and so were willing to support the king in acquiring additional power as head of the church. For the rest of the Tudor period it was the sovereign or, during Edward VI's reign, those ruling on his behalf, who controlled policy, and in large measure represented the wishes of the majority of Englishmen.

The Act of Supremacy, 1534, made the king Supreme Head of the Church in England, and therefore vested in him a sovereignty as absolute as that of the Pope. He decided which of his children should succeed him on the throne. His immediate heir was to be his son Prince Edward. Next in line Henry nominated Mary, his older daughter by Catherine of Aragon, and finally Elizabeth, his younger daughter by Anne Boleyn.

Catholics considered that Elizabeth was illegitimate, and that therefore Mary Stuart, Queen of Scots, and the great-grand-daughter of Henry VII, had a superior and legitimate claim to the throne by hereditary right, a fact used by opponents of Elizabeth.

Against this, to safeguard the position of Elizabeth, Parliament passed a law excluding the Scottish line from the succession, and a law of Elizabeth's Parliament made it high treason to question the right of Parliament to alter the succession.

In reality, the vital factor throughout most of the Tudor period was the monarch himself, and the personal system of government which the Tudor kings and queens maintained. They believed that they ruled by divine right, but they did not harp upon the theory. They hated opposition: Henry VIII punished it ruthlessly, while Elizabeth could be both imperious and tactful; but they generally followed policies which were popular with at least a large section of their more influential subjects. They consulted Parliament frequently, and were able to keep on friendly terms with it, partly because they ensured that many of its members were their supporters, whose interests were advanced by the measures they advocated, (Edward VI, Mary and Elizabeth made or revived sixty-three boroughs which returned one hundred and twenty-three royal nominees to the Commons), partly because they stood for law and order at home, security from foreign enemies, and conditions which enabled the rising middle class to increase their wealth.

They governed mainly through a Privy Council whose members they appointed, and from whom they chose their chief ministers. The Privy Council could advise, but with no certainty that their advice would be taken. Ministers were not members of Parliament, and were not responsible to Parliament.

17 Henry VII Chapel, Westminster Abbey

All the Tudor monarchs had strongly individualistic personalities, and all contributed important strands to the character of the English monarchy.

Henry VII was mean, thin-faced and cunning, but his thrifty economic policy enabled him to build up a large royal fortune which greatly strengthened the position of the crown, whilst at the same time he reduced the power of the barons, and ensured that the lawlessness of the Wars of the Roses would not return. He has been called 'the cleverest king who ever sat on the throne of England'. Although he appeared mean, he was not miserly: having acquired great wealth, he was willing to spend it on music and fine church building. By avoiding war and encouraging trade, he set England on the road to unity, wealth and power.

Henry VIII enormously increased the popularity of the monarchy, by his skill in sport, his 'prince charming' appearance, his sturdy opposition to papal influence in England, and his determination to increase the international power and reputation of England. At the same time, his ruthless treatment of those who opposed him, or failed to carry out his wishes, aroused mingled fear and respect, for his main course of action usually seemed to his subjects to be in the public interest.

Elizabeth's intense love of England, and her quite unscrupulous use of the services of her admirers enabled her to unite most of the English people against the threat of foreign attack. She raised loyalty to the sovereign to one of the highest points it has reached, while her practical, unbiassed attitude to religion helped England to avoid the religious civil wars that devastated much of Europe.

Throughout the Tudor period the final freedom of England from papal interference was still not assured. To counter the claims of the Pope that he alone ruled by the will of God, English writers and clerics asserted that the English State was also a manifestation of God's will, and since the sovereign was the most important element in the State, they elaborated the doctrine of the Divine Right of Kings.

Factors determining the Succession

The statute declaring Elizabeth queen, stated 'Your Highness is rightly, lineally and lawfully descended and come out of the blood royal of this Realm of England in and to . . . whose princely person . . . the imperial and royal estate, place, crown and dignity are and shall be most fully . . . invested and incorporated.' At the same time the statute stated that Elizabeth's accession was in accordance with the Act of Parliament which had ratified Henry VIII's will with regard to the succession.

In 1570, the Pope excommunicated Elizabeth and called for her deposition. The reply by Bullinger was that the Pope was usurping the rights granted to kings by God. In defence of the queen, her right to rule was shown to be the result of divine decree, but since Mary, Queen of Scots, was still alive as the nearest legitimate heir and claimed to be the rightful ruler of England, Bullinger argued that the succession to the throne was elective, and in the hands of the State. The

28   **18** Portrait of Queen Elizabeth I in 1558, from the Queen's Bench Plea Roll

Word of God, he added, gave support to the organisation of society by kings, and by the parliaments and other means through which they ruled.

From this theory of the God-given right of the king to rule as he thought fit, was derived the idea that the subject must show absolute obedience to the sovereign; to rebel against the king was to rebel against God. Complete obedience, wrote Bishop Jewell in Elizabeth's reign, was due not only to princes, but to the magistrates they appointed, even 'though they be very wicked'.

Shakespeare expressed the sixteenth century conception of kingship: it was the supreme example of the orderliness of God's creation, the force which kept mankind from relapsing into chaos.

> The heavens themselves, the planets, and this centre,
> Observe degree, priority, and place
>
> . . . .
>
> And therefore is the glorious planet, Sol,
> In noble eminence enthron'd and spher'd
> Amidst the other; whose med'cinable eye
> Corrects the ill aspects of planets evil,
> And posts, like the commandment of a king,
> Sans check, to good and bad: but when the planets
> In evil mixture, to disorder wander,
> What plagues, and what portents! what mutiny!
>
> . . . .
>
>   O, when degree is shak'd,
> Which is the ladder to all high designs,
> The enterprise is sick.
>
> . . . .
>
> Then everything includes itself in power,
> Power into will, will into appetite;
> And appetite, a universal wolf,
> So doubly seconded with will and power,
> Must make perforce a universal prey,
> And, last, eat up himself.

The king's main function was to sustain and maintain the God-given structure of society, the hierarchy, of influence and power. 'Degree', the ordered arrangement of society, was vital: each man in his proper class, each class in its proper place in the hierarchy. Each man and each class had its rights and its duties; and the king had supreme rights over his subjects, and also supreme responsibility towards them. The monarch thus gave unity and permanence to the whole graded system.

To question this order led to ruinous power-politics and chaos. Since God had ordained this disciplined and ordered society, he must also ordain that obedience

29

19 Gold Coins of King James I

to the monarch is the supreme duty of the subject; as the Archbishop of Canterbury says in *King Henry V*:

> Therefore doth heaven divide
> The state of man in divers functions,
> Setting endeavour in continual motion;
> To which is fixed, as an aim or butt,
> Obedience.

Better a bad king than the disorder which 'rends the unity and married calm of states'. In *King John* the king speaks of 'the free breath of a sacred king', sacred, no matter how lacking the king may be in the qualities of good kingship.

To their supporters, the individual qualities of rival claimants to the throne in the sixteenth century were less important than their religion. The papal supporters of Mary, Queen of Scots, had based claims to the English throne on the fact that she was the nearest legitimate heir, but after her execution, her son James VI of Scotland inherited her claim. But he was a Protestant, and the papal writers suddenly ceased to emphasise the importance of direct inheritance, and stated that 'the succession to government by nearness of blood is not by law of Nature and Divine'. The anti-papal writers, on the other hand, emphasised it still more. The English Parliament was now converted to the importance of hereditary succession, and on the death of Elizabeth, in spite of previous Acts excluding the Scottish line, unanimously accepted James Stuart, King of Scotland, the nearest heir, as King of England.

4 The Early Stuarts

Kings will be tyrants from policy, when
subjects are rebels from principle.
E. BURKE, *Reflections on the Revolution in France.*

Laws are vain, by which we right enjoy
If Kings unquestioned can those laws destroy.
DRYDEN, 'Absolom and Achitophel'.

James I

The Statute recognising the title of James I carefully avoided any statement that Parliament was granting the throne to James, but merely declared:

.... 'a most joyful and just recognition of the immediate, lawful and undoubted succession of Descent and Right of the Crown.

We, (being bounden thereunto both by the laws of God and man) do recognise and acknowledge (and thereby express our unspeakable joys) that immediately upon the dissolution and decease of Elizabeth . . . the imperial crown of the realm of England, did, by inherent birthright and lawful and undoubted succession descend and come to your most excellent majesty, as being lineally, justly and lawfully next and sole heir of the blood royal of this realm as is aforesaid.

There was therefore considerable justification for James I's claim that he ruled by Divine Right, for his unanimous welcome to England was based entirely on the fact that he was the nearest heir, and this in spite of two earlier Acts of Parliament excluding the House of Stuart.

James knew little of the laws and liberties of England. In spite of their belief in their God-given power, the Tudor sovereigns showed great respect for the customary law. One of James's first acts was something Henry VIII or Elizabeth would not have thought of doing – he had a thief executed without trial. James's conception of Divine Right was more autocratic than that of the Tudors, but by the time of his accession, opinions on the relative power of king and Parliament were changing.

The circumstances which had led Parliament to support the idea of Divine Right were now different. The threat of papal interference had diminished, and whereas Parliament had no objection to the king increasing his power at the expense of the clergy, they had no wish to lose their own powers, but rather wished to increase them.

James read his first Parliament a lecture on the divine power of the Crown, and told the members of the Commons that they were allowed to meet only by

20 King James I in Parliament

his gracious favour. This of course was resented by Parliament who told the king that he had been misinformed on the matter.

The judges, who were appointed by the Crown, agreed with the king's view, and stated 'whatever is due by the law or constitution of man may be altered; but natural legiance or obedience of the subject to the sovereign cannot be altered.'

James himself wrote, 'As it is atheism and blasphemy to dispute what God can do, so it is a presumption and a high contempt in a subject to dispute what a king can do, or to say that a king cannot do this or that.'

The leading clergy of the Church of England feared the growing influence of the Puritans, and firmly supported the king. In 1604 James called a conference of Puritans, who raised the question of the abolition of bishops. At once James showed that he realised how closely at that time the royal power was connected with, indeed dependent upon that of the church. 'No bishop, no king,' he said, and threatened to harry the Puritans out of the kingdom. 'In two minutes,' says the historian Gardener, 'he had sealed his own fate and that of England for ever.' Meanwhile the bishops realised how important it was to secure the support of the king.

After 1611 James made little use of Parliament. Government was carried on by the King's favourites whom the great lords of the Council hated as upstarts. James thus destroyed the friendly co-operation between the Crown and both Houses of Parliament, which had worked so well during the Tudor period. He died in 1625, and Charles I inherited much of the opposition his father had engendered. He did little to placate it.

Charles I

There were frequent disputes between king and Parliament, the king claiming that Parliament had no right to take any part in government unless asked to do so, and Parliament claiming that the country was governed by 'the king in Parliament', and that no taxes could be levied without the consent of Parliament. Ever since 1407 the House of Commons had had the power to initiate Bills involving the grant of public money and the imposition of taxation.

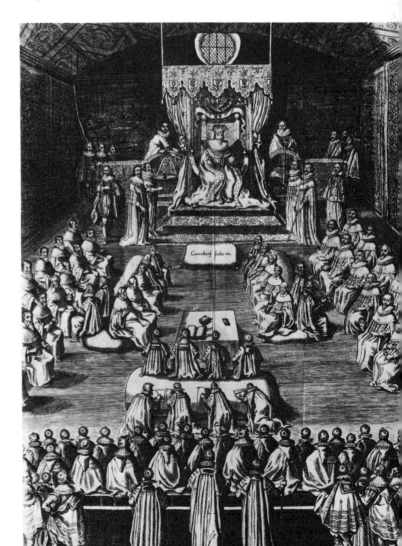

21 King Charles I opening Parliament, 1625. The commons are presenting their Speaker to the King

Growing Parliamentary Claims During the first three years of Charles I's reign, England was at war with first Spain and then France, and the king called Parliament to obtain the necessary money. Parliament refused to vote money for the war, and so Charles dissolved it. A second Parliament demanded the impeachment of the king's favourite and minister, Buckingham. To save him, Charles dissolved his second Parliament. The war was going badly and in 1628 Charles was forced to call another Parliament. This time Parliament presented the king with the Petition of Right, promising a large sum of money if Charles would agree to it. The main points of the petition were that the king should not levy any taxes or forced loans without the consent of Parliament, that no man should be imprisoned without trial and no civilian tried by a military court. The king agreed; but when Parliament went on to demand the dismissal of Buckingham, the King dismissed it.

'I must let you know,' he said, 'that I will not allow any of my servants to be questioned among you, much less such as one of eminent place and near me. . . . Remember that parliaments are altogether in my power for their calling, sitting and dissolution, and therefore, as I find the fruits of them good or evil, they are to continue or not to be.'

At their next session early in 1629, Parliament demanded control of church affairs. They passed the Three Resolutions, declaring that anyone who (1) tried to bring Roman Catholic practices into the Church of England, or (2) advised the levying of a tax not agreed by Parliament, or (3) paid such a tax, was an enemy to the kingdom. The Speaker was afraid to put the resolutions, and tried to close the sitting, but angry members held him down in his chair while the resolutions were passed.

Rule without Parliament Charles believed that his divine right as king gave him the unlimited right to rule as he thought best, and that promises given to Parliament need not be kept. He therefore decided to rule without calling Parliament at all, and ignored the Petition of Right. Sir John Eliot and two other parliamentary leaders were put in prison, and Sir John Eliot was kept there until he died.

For the next eleven years, Charles ruled as he believed God meant him to rule, and there is good evidence that he was more sympathetic to the poorer people than the wealthy land owners, lawyers and merchants who composed Parliament, had been. He imposed such taxes as he thought right, and aroused much opposition from the wealthy who felt they were being forced to pay more than they should. He imprisoned merchants who refused to pay taxes not agreed by Parliament. There were no means of opposing the king, for public meetings were not allowed, and no books or newspapers could be published without the permission of the king and the bishops. Men who dared to write pamphlets criticising the bishops were tried in the Court of the Star Chamber and condemned to have their ears or tongues or right hand cut off.

The bishops continued to support the king and his views of government. In

1640 they issued a statement: 'The most high and sacred order of kings is of Divine Right, being the ordinance of God Himself, founded in the prime laws of nature and clearly established by express texts both of the Old and New Testaments. A supreme power is given to this most excellent order by God Himself in the Scripture, which is that kings should rule and command in their several dominions all persons of what rank or estate soever, . . . For any person or persons to set up maintain or avow . . . any independent co-active power . . . is treasonable against God as well as against their Kings.'

Churchmen, led by Archbishop Laud, supported the idea of the Divine Right of Kings as the lesser of two evils. The king was well disposed to the system of church government by bishops, but the Puritans were hostile to the very existence of Bishops. Parliament seemed to be coming increasingly under the influence of the Puritans, and the clergy therefore had no wish to see the king's power curtailed by Parliament.

The king and his chief supporter, Archbishop Laud, thus alienated the sympathies of both the wealthy and the Puritans, of the landowners and the merchants. Many of the poor believed that the king was their friend. He tried to enforce the fixing of wages at a reasonable rate, and the payment of poor relief. He also tried

22 Disturbances in the High Church, Edinburgh, in opposition to the English Prayer Book and Church Services

to save for the villagers their common land and rights by stopping the enclosures by wealthy landowners. When the clash came between the king and his critics, however, the poor had little influence.

Towards the end of his eleven year period of rule without Parliament, Charles proceeded to anger yet another section of his subjects.

As was commonly held in those days, Charles believed that it was part of the king's duty to decide the religion of all his subjects, and in 1638 he tried to force upon the Scots the prayer book and service of the Church of England. The Scots refused and war broke out but the king had insufficient money to raise any adequate force to oppose them.

Thomas Wentworth, Earl of Strafford, the king's most efficient minister, hurried back from Ireland, supervised the raising of troops and advised the calling of Parliament.

The king's difficulty was Parliament's opportunity: when the king asked for money for the war, this was refused and Charles dissolved Parliament. There were riots, but the leaders were put to death, and some members of Parliament were imprisoned. The king and Strafford tried to raise money by forced loans, and London aldermen who refused to subscribe were imprisoned.

The Long Parliament   Such troops as were raised, with the help of press-gangs, were mutinous. The Scots invaded England and captured Newcastle. They demanded a large sum of money and a promise that there should be no interference with the religion of Scotland. There was nothing for it but to call another Parliament. It met in October 1640 and is known as the Long Parliament.

Under its leader, John Pym, a wealthy business man, Parliament drew up an impeachment of Strafford. Charles assured him that he could safely come to London, but when he went to take his place in the House of Lords, he was met with angry shouts of 'Withdraw!' A man who was impeached could not sit in the Lords.

Meanwhile the queen was appealing to the Pope, and to French Catholics for help, and plotting with army officers for a march on London to release Strafford. Commons and Lords then passed a Bill of Attainder, condemning Strafford to death. The king's signature only was needed. Crowds surrounded the palace all night, calling for Strafford's death. Charles had given his word that he would ensure Strafford's safety, but now he feared for the safety of the queen and the royal family. All day he hesitated. The crowds grew larger and angrier and at last he gave way, and signed the death warrant of his ablest and most loyal minister. It was an act which he regretted to the end of his life.

Charles' will to resist seemed to have gone with the execution of Strafford, and he agreed to a series of radical measures. One Bill enacted that the Long Parliament could not be dissolved without its own consent. Parliament then went on to demand the right to control taxation, the choice of the king's ministers, and the abolition of the special courts, such as the Courts of the Star Chamber and of

23 King Charles I demands the handing over of the Five Members

High Commission where the king's and the archbishops' critics could be punished.

For a time almost all members of Parliament were united against the king, but when the Puritans in Parliament attacked the organisation of the Church of England by proposing the abolition of the bishops, there was a great difference of opinion. The Puritan leaders in Parliament proposed that the control of the army should be taken from the king and vested in Parliament but many members had no wish to see the Puritans in control of the army – they would prefer it to be in the hands of the king.

Charles felt that he had enough support to take the offensive. He ordered the Attorney General to impeach in the House of Lords, five leading members of the Commons, but the Lords considered an impeachment by the king to be illegal, and refused to arrest the five members. Next day, Charles himself, went to the House of Commons to arrest them. This was a breach of Parliament's privilege and as Charles left the Chamber, the members shouted 'Privilege, Privilege', while the King's supporters brandished their weapons at the open doorway. The five members had escaped to the City of London where they were safe. A large number of armed men marched up from Buckinghamshire to protect John Hampden, their member of Parliament. Charles withdrew from London to York. Both sides began to prepare forces for possible Civil War.

5 Civil War, the Interregnum and the Restoration

Tis hard for kings to steer an equal course
And they who banish one oft gain a worse.
DRYDEN 'Tarquin and Tullia'.

Yet know that Kings are gods on earth
And thou that pull them down
Shall find it is no less than death
To tamper with a Crown.
A Short history of the English Rebellion, 1660, MARCHMOND NEDHAM.

The Civil War – The Supporters of the King and Parliament

The war started in the summer of 1642. Charles maintained that he was fighting rebels who were guilty of treason against his divine right to rule as he thought fit. The Parliamentarians claimed to be fighting for the true interests of the king against his evil advisers. The issue was whether Britain was to be ruled by a despotic king as was becoming the case in most parts of Europe, or whether she was to be ruled by a Parliament of elected members. It was certainly not a case of the king against the people, for most of the people had no more say in the election of members of Parliament than they had in the choice of a king. Nor was it a case of the rich against the poor, or the workers against the employers. About two-thirds of the members of the Commons fought against the king, and one-third of the Lords. The House of Commons was said to be much richer than the House of Lords and though most of the very big landowners were on the side of the king, many others and the wealthy merchants, and traders, were on the side of Parliament, together with their apprentices. Farmers who rented their land usually found it wise to follow their landlords, but yeoman freeholders in the east and midlands were mainly for Parliament, those in the west and north for the king. Many country gentlemen were found on each side.

It was on religious grounds that the people were most clearly divided. The Catholics almost all supported the king, and so did the bishops and the members of the Church of England who favoured Archbishop Laud's ideas, but the more puritanical members of the Church of England and the Independents and other Puritan sects were for Parliament.

Some men who sympathised with the Puritans and with Parliament nevertheless felt that they could not betray the loyalty they felt was due to the king, and fought for him. As Sir Edmund Verney said, 'I have eaten the king's bread and served him for thirty years, and will not do so base a thing as forsake him: I choose rather to lose my life – which I am sure I shall do – to preserve and defend those things which are against my conscience to preserve and defend.'

By 1646 almost all the king's forces were defeated, and Charles surrendered. The Parliamentary leaders now tried to come to an arrangement with Charles, ensuring him the crown, provided that he accepted that most of the power of government should be retained by Parliament.

Charles, however, was trying to encourage the growing disagreements between his enemies, in the hope that some of them would join him. Most members of Parliament were anxious for an agreement with the king, but many of the army leaders were not, while many of the rank and file were demanding a republic and votes for all men.

In 1647, making promises he had no intention of keeping, and assuring the English Parliament that he had no intention of any such action, Charles persuaded the Scots to support him, and he renewed the Civil war.

The King's Trial and Execution

The Parliamentary army led by Cromwell easily crushed the royalist forces but all faith in the King's trustworthiness, and in any hopes of peace while the king remained alive were rapidly vanishing in some of the Parliamentary leaders. They prepared to bring 'Charles Stuart, that Man of blood' to public trial for treason against his subjects. The members of Parliament who were unwilling to do this were excluded from Parliament by Colonel Pride and his soldiers, leaving only 'the Rump' as it was called. It contained less than a quarter of the original House of Commons.

Kings had been deposed, imprisoned and murdered before this, but no king had ever been brought before a court of law, accused of treason and condemned to death, yet this is what the 'Rump' of Parliament proceeded to do. The small band of men left from the House of Commons which had been elected in 1640 chose a court composed of some of their members, an Irish and a Scottish Lord, eleven baronets, army officers, and some mayors and leading citizens of London and other towns. When Charles was brought before them, he refused to plead, saying that no man in England could be tried save by his peers (equals) and that therefore no court could be formed which could try a king. He denied that the so-called court had any legal rights or existence.

This was true, but Cromwell and his fellow members were convinced that new

24 The House of Commons in 1648

25　*Top left* King Charles I at his trial

26　*Top Right:* The Execution of Charles I, from a contemporary broadsheet

27　*Below:* King Charles I, from his Apologia, published on the day of his funeral

times and new situations required new procedures, but they tried to give the trial as good an appearance of legality as they could, and condemned Charles to death. They made no attempt to conduct the trial in secrecy, but threw it open for the world to see – they believed that it was through the Will of God that they had triumphed, and that they, and not the king, now ruled by Divine Right. The 'Rump' resolved that 'the office of king in this nation is unnecessary, burthensome, and dangerous. . . . That the People are, under God, the original of all just power; that the Commons of England in Parliament assembled being chosen by, and representing the People, have the supreme power in the nation. . . .'

'What King's Majesty,' wrote John Milton, 'sitting on an exalted throne, ever shone so brightly as that of the people of England then did, when, shaking off that old superstition which had prevailed a long time, they gave judgment on the king himself, or rather on an enemy that had been their king, caught as it were, in a net by his own laws, and scrupled not to inflict on him, being guilty, the same punishment which he would have inflicted on any other? . . . We went on in no obscure but an illustrious passage, pointed out and made plain to us by God himself.'

The Lord Protector

The popular belief in 'the divinity that doth hedge a king', was not so easily overthrown, and many of those who had fought against the king had no sympathy with the 'Regicides'. The Rump and the leaders of the army lost much of the support of the people. In Scotland and Ireland, Charles's son was immediately proclaimed King Charles II, but in England the army and the Rump Parliament had control, and the people's sympathy for the king had little effect.

Cromwell led an army to Ireland and then to Scotland, and the supporters of Charles II were defeated. The whole of the British Isles was united in the Commonwealth. For a time the Rump of the Long Parliament continued to rule, but

28 The First Seal of the Commonwealth, dated A.D. 1648

the country was threatened with disruption: the army, the defeated royalists, the Rump, the various religious groups – Independents, Levellers, Presbyterians and others, all were scheming to increase their power. If it had been one man, King Charles, who had brought disunity to the country, it also seemed that it needed one man to restore some sort of unity, and by 1653 it was clear that Cromwell, who had led the army to victory and had taken a leading part in the execution of Charles, was the only man who could do so. He was appointed Lord Protector and although he had fought in order to keep Parliamentary government, and although he honestly tried to govern with the help of Parliament, he was soon dismissing Parliaments, and ruling more dictatorially than even Charles had done. By 1657 the leading men in the country were asking him to accept the title of king. This he refused to do, but he nominated his son Richard as Protector to succeed him, as though he were king, and the founder of a new royal family.

Charles II

Again the country was faced with dissension through the rivalries of the army leaders, for Richard had not his father's strength of personality and he resigned. The bulk of the people were tired of Parliamentary and army squabbles and of puritan dictators, and when General Monk, commander of the army in Scotland called a convention in London in 1660, it was overwhelmingly agreed to ask Charles II to come to England and resume the crown. In the difficult circumstances of the times, kingship proved to be the most satisfactory method of securing peaceful rule. There was little opposition and Charles wisely abstained from revenging his father's death by hunting down all the leading men who had supported Parliament. A dozen men who had signed Charles I's death warrant were executed and the rotting bodies of Cromwell, Ireton and Bradshaw were dug up, hanged, and decapitated, but that was all.

The powers of the king, however, were not those that Charles I had claimed. A Parliament of landowners, lawyers and merchants had tasted power, and they would never relinquish it. Charles II knew that he was king on sufferance, and while he skilfully manipulated affairs and accepted money from Louis XIV of France to avoid having to go cap in hand too often to Parliament, he was careful not to risk having to 'go on his travels again'.

He made a secret treaty with Louis XIV by which England was to help France in an attack on Holland and Louis was to help Charles to restore the Roman Catholic religion in England. Charles issued a Declaration of Indulgence giving freedom of worship to both Catholics and Dissenters (Puritans or Non-Conformists who would not accept the Church of England). Parliament, however, passed an Act forbidding the holding of office in the government or army by anyone who was not a member of the Church of England. The war went badly, and William of Orange, Charles's nephew, became head of the Dutch government. Parliament demanded that the war should end. Charles decided that the Catholics were not likely to be of much use to him in increasing his power and he then looked for support from the members of the Church of England. He made the Earl of Danby his chief minister. Danby began to build up a party in Parliament who would support the king. It was called the Court Party, and its members came to be called Tories. Those who opposed the Tories formed the Country Party and were soon known as Whigs.

In 1678 rumours of a Roman Catholic plot were spread by a man named Titus Oates. The Catholics were said to be planning the murder of Charles and the conquest of England with French and Irish troops. Panic followed. Many Catholics were tried and put to death and Parliament introduced an Exclusion Bill to prevent Charles's brother, James, who was a Catholic, from succeeding to the throne. Charles dissolved Parliament, but they had already passed the *Habeas Corpus* Act, demanding that no man should be kept in prison without trial.

The next Parliament introduced another Exclusion Bill which was passed by the Commons but rejected by the Lords. Charles called the next Parliament at Oxford instead of London, where Parliament always had the support of the citizens. A third Exclusion Bill was introduced, and Parliament hoped that Charles's need of money would force him to accept it. But the king did not need their money – he had just received a large sum from Louis XIV and he dissolved Parliament after a few days.

Some of the Whigs began to plot rebellion, but they were betrayed and the leaders executed. If the king did not want to go on his travels again, most of the people certainly did not want to be involved in civil war again, and so they were prepared to allow the king to take more power into his hands and those of his Tory party. There was still considerable support for the idea of the King's Divine Right. In 1681 the University of Cambridge, in an address to Charles stated,

We still believe and maintain, that our Kings derive not their title from the people, but from God; that to Him only they are accountable; that it belongs not to subjects either to create or censure, but to honour and obey their sovereign, who comes to be so by a fundamental hereditary right of succession, which no religion, no law, no fault or forfeiture can alter or diminish.

Charles decided to rule without Parliament. Charters of towns were taken away and the King's friends given control. Before serious opposition could arise, he died in 1685.

6 The Glorious Revolution and Constitutional Monarchy

The king reigns, but does not govern.
JAN ZAMOYSKI (1541–1605) Speech in Polish Parliament, 1605

James II

The Tory party controlled Parliament and they enthusiastically welcomed James II as king, and granted him large sums of taxation for life. With so many powerful Church of England Tory friends, James felt that he was in a very strong position. In June 1685 the Protestant Duke of Monmouth landed at Lyme Regis with a few followers. The peasants from the countryside near joined him and he was proclaimed king at Taunton. His small army was poorly equipped and led and was soon routed by James's army at the Battle of Sedgemoor. Hundreds of fugitives were hunted down, captured and hanged by Judge Jeffreys at the Bloody Assize. Monmouth was executed and Jeffreys rewarded by being made Lord Chancellor.

James's Tory supporters had believed that he would be satisfied to practise his Catholic religion privately, but encouraged by the ease with which Monmouth had been disposed of James began appointing Catholics to important positions

29 The seven Bishops being taken to the Tower

in the government and the army, in spite of the law stating that only members of the Church of England could hold these positions.

When Parliament asked for a reduction in the army and the dismissal of Catholic officers, James dissolved it, and issued another Declaration of Indulgence, allowing non-members of the Church of England to be appointed to important positions. Seven bishops who refused to read the Declaration were brought to trial on a charge of treason. When they were acquitted, there was widespread rejoicing.

In 1688 a son was born to James, and it appeared that there might be a succession of Catholic kings. The Whigs, who had already been corresponding with James's daughter, Mary and her husband, William of Orange, were joined by most of the Tory leaders, and William was invited to invade England. William landed and all the leading men flocked to support him. James fled ignominiously to France.

30 Broadsheet, 1688, Great and Good News of the Church to England

James had been king for only three years, but three years of attempts to use the royal power to subvert the laws on religion, and to build up an army to support his Roman Catholic ambitions were enough to turn almost the whole country against him. But this time there was no suggestion that Britain could do without a king. If the direct hereditary line was unsatisfactory, then the next in line must be approached, and Mary, James's Protestant daughter and her Dutch husband, William of Orange became joint sovereigns.

The Settlement of 1688

William was anxious to gain the support of England in his struggle to stop the aggressive plans of Louis XIV of France, which were threatening Holland. He was quite willing to accept the limitations which Parliament wished to place upon the power of the sovereign, in exchange for this. The requirements of Parliament were embodied in the Bill of Rights. Parliament was to be freely elected and its members were to have freedom of speech; no taxation could be imposed without the consent of Parliament: the king had no power to suspend any law; an army could be raised or maintained only with Parliament's consent and this had to be renewed annually. No Roman Catholic could succeed to the throne of Britain. Parliament also decided that the king's revenue could be granted

31 Broadsheet, Popery's Downfall and The Protestants Uprising

for a year only and so this ensured the annual meeting of Parliament. The Triennial Act ordered a General Election every three years. The Commons denied the right of the Lords to amend any money Bill, and enacted that money could be spent only for the purpose for which it was voted.

The Act of Settlement

The Act of Settlement, 1701, confirmed Parliament's claim to decide upon the succession to the throne. All Roman Catholic claimants were barred from the throne which was to be settled after the death of William (Mary had died in 1694) first upon Princess Anne and then upon the Electress Sophia and her son, George, the Protestant line descended from James I's daughter who had married the German Elector Palatine.

Parliament therefore, while barring the unacceptable Roman Catholic Stuarts, accepted that thereafter the principle of Primogeniture should be followed. This principle has both advantages and disadvantages. It ensures that there is only one legitimate claimant to the throne and very much lessens the likelihood of rival claims leading to civil war. The heir can be educated from childhood in preparation for kingship (not always done, and not necessarily an advantage, if the reigning monarch's ideas of kingship leave much to be desired). A sole heir will not need to build up a party of supporters, who will expect to be rewarded on his accession, nor need he try to win public favour by spectacular shows of little real value, as might be the case where there were several claimants.

On the other hand, it is unlikely that any royal family would continue to produce a constant succession of intelligent and gifted eldest sons. In fact, royal sons have often been very different from their royal fathers. As Kingsley Martin says – 'the gay Monarch was the son of the pious Charles I. George III always domesticated, even when insane, followed his heavily amorous grandfather, George II. George IV again was the most notorious libertine.'

In the days when kings had great power, this failure to inherit good qualities

47

was a big risk, and frequently led to periods of disastrous rule, but when the monarch's powers are limited as they are today, the damage that a weak and irresponsible king might do, is also limited.

The Act of Settlement established the principle that ministers, though chosen by the king, were ultimately responsible to Parliament. They were also responsible for advising the king, and as time passed, they came to accept responsibility for the sovereign's actions. Hence arose the convention that 'the king can do no wrong'. This really meant that the king was expected to accept his ministers' advice, and so without their agreement, could do nothing at all.

The king's power was further limited – he could no longer dismiss judges who could now be removed from office only by the Law Courts, or by the two houses of Parliament; the king could not pardon a minister impeached by the House of Commons, but he still continued to select the ministers and he could veto a Bill brought in in Parliament.

The troubles of the seventeenth century had proved that the only satisfactory government for Britain at that time appeared to be a Monarchy, but that it was also essential that the monarchy must be limited by Parliament.

The Crown, besides appointing ministers, still had a great deal of control over home and foreign policy, but William was so occupied with the latter, and his leadership in the coalition of European States against Louis XIV, that home affairs were left mainly to his ministers.

He had no wish to form a King's Party in Parliament, and took his ministers from both Whigs and Tories, and many leaders continued to intrigue with the exiled James II. There was much opposition to his policy, and Parliament insisted on a reduction in the size of the army. At one time the opposition was so great that William thought of resigning the crown. A small group of wealthy and powerful families controlled the country. They had saved England from unlimited monarchy: they substituted almost unlimited oligarchy.

Louis XIV refused to recognise William as King of England until the Peace of Ryswick in 1697. When James II died in 1701, however, Louis recognised James's son, known as the 'Old Pretender' as James III, King of England. This aroused enthusiastic support for William's renewal of the war, and although William died in 1702, the government continued his policy, and the War of the Spanish Succession occupied most of the new reign.

Queen Anne

Princess Anne succeeded to the throne, in accordance with the terms of the Bill of Rights. During her reign there was bitter strife between Whigs and Tories for the control of policy. The first ministry contained both Whigs and Tories, but gradually the Tories increased opposition to the War, and withdrew from the government.

Queen Anne was at first much influenced by the Duchess of Marlborough, whose husband, John Churchill, Duke of Marlborough, was the brilliant com-

33 Coin with Portrait of Queen Anne

mander of the army in the war on the Continent. About 1708, the Duchess quarrelled with the Queen and her place was taken by Mrs Masham, a supporter of the Tories. The Queen had already shown signs of a growing dislike for the Whigs, and when a Dr Sacheverell, preached a sermon attacking the Whig members and suggesting that their policy was endangering the unity of the Church of England, she was very concerned. When the government impeached Dr Sacheverell, he became a public hero. The Queen then dismissed the Whigs and appointed Tory Ministers. Parliament was dissolved, and the new House of Commons had a large Tory majority.

All Queen Anne's children had died, and when the succession to the throne was considered, a peaceful solution appeared very unlikely. The Electress Sophia

34 Queen Anne and the Touch of Royalty. It was thought that the monarch had the power to heal sufferers by touching them

and her son were Germans and unknown in England. Most of the Tories would have preferred a Stuart succession, but they were also great supporters of the Church of England. The Old Pretender refused to change his Roman Catholic religion and the Tories hesitated. The Queen was taken suddenly ill, and some Whig Dukes swayed the decision of the Council, and on the Queen's death, George, Elector of Hanover, was proclaimed king. Some Tory squires continued to toast 'the King across the water', but most people in England quickly accepted the Hanoverian succession.

In Scotland there was an attempt to restore the House of Stuart. The Scots had not accepted the English Settlement of Succession after the Revolution of 1688, and in 1703, the Scottish Parliament passed an Act of Security by which they would accept the accession of Anne only if England agreed to free trade with Scotland and allowed them to control their own affairs. This Act was vetoed by Queen Anne, but the following year a similar Act of Security was accepted by her.

In 1603 the crowns of England and Scotland had been united. In 1707 it was agreed that the Parliaments too should join together, so that there was now one kingdom of Great Britain, with one sovereign and one Parliament.

Not all the Scots, however, were willing to accept George I as king, and there was a rebellion, largely among the Highlanders, in 1715, but it was easily suppressed.

7 The Early Hanoverians

God bless the King, I mean the Faith's Defender,
God bless – no harm in blessing – the Pretender
But who Pretender is, or who is King
God bless us all – that's quite another thing.
               JOHN BYROM (1692–1763) *To an Officer in the Army*

Wha the de'il hae we got for a King
But a wee wee German Lairdie
     ALLAN CUNNINGHAM (1784–1842) *The wee wee German Lairdie.*

George the First was reckoned vile –
Viler still was George the Second;
And what mortal ever heard
Any good of George the Third?
When to hell the Fourth descended,
Heaven be praised, the Georges ended.

George I and George II

The Hanoverian succession had an important effect upon the position of the king. George I could not speak English, and George II spoke it badly, so they did not attend the meetings of their Council of Ministers. It therefore became the custom for one of the ministers to preside. Gradually the presiding minister instead of the king came to appoint other ministers, and he became known as the Prime Minister. As the king had not been at the meeting, and as he knew little or nothing about the system of government in Britain, he was usually ready to accept the minister's advice, both as to policy and as to the appointment of ministers. The king no longer used the right to veto a Bill passed by Parliament. What George I did do, however, was to ensure as much wealth as he could for himself and his friends and retinue. 'A flight of hungry Hanoverians' wrote Lord Mahon, 'like so many famished vultures, fell with keen eyes and bended talons on the fruitful soil of England.' 'The German women plundered,' said Thackeray, 'the German secretaries plundered, the German cooks and attendants plundered; even Mustapha and Mahomet, the German negroes, had a share in the booty.'

Parliament had to grant £1,300,000 to meet George I's debts, and many large sums to cover George III's expense accounts, but this was a cheap price to pay for a royal family who left the ruling families in undisputed power; for the loss of power by the king was not a gain in power for the people generally. Eighteenth century Britain was ruled by a small number of wealthy landowners and their friends who controlled the elections to Parliament and occupied the positions of

36 King George I as a Roman Emperor, a bust by John Rysbrack

importance. In so far as the king could exert any influence, it was merely substituting some of the aristocracy for others.

George III

George III, grandson of George II, was educated in Britain and said he 'gloried in the name of Briton'. It is said that his German mother repeatedly said to him, 'George, be a King,' and he determined that he would take a much greater share in governing than George I and George II had done. Many Tories supported him in this, and many of them in the House of Commons, were known as the 'King's Friends', always ready to act according to his wishes. He did not wish to take away the power of Parliament but aimed at gaining control of Parliament through a King's Party. The leading politicians were far from united, and the king was able to play off one against another. During the first ten years of his reign, he chose several Prime Ministers in succession, but none quite suited his wishes.

Under Grenville began the tactless handling of the discontent in the American Colonies. Grenville objected strongly to criticism of the king's government, particularly that of John Wilkes, a member of Parliament who wrote in the *North Briton*. The Government issued a general warrant for the arrest of authors, printers and publishers of the *North Briton*, but Wilkes claimed that as a member of Parliament he could not be arrested for libel, but he was expelled from member-

37 The House of Commons during Sir Robert Walpole's administration. Walpole on the left, Earl Onslow in centre, clerk of the House of Commons on the right

ship of the House. In 1768 Wilkes was elected as member of Parliament for Middlesex. The government declared that he could not sit, and ordered fresh elections. Wilkes stood again and was again elected, to the slogan of 'Wilkes and Liberty'. Three times he was expelled and three times re-elected. Then Parliament declared his opponent elected although he obtained only 296 votes to Wilkes's 1143. There was such an outcry that the king had to accept the government's resignation.

In 1770 Lord North was appointed Prime Minister. He was easy-going, and quite prepared to leave a great deal of the government to the king, who on two occasions, summoned a cabinet meeting himself and presided over it. He vetoed his ministers' proposals, and made many appointments in the army, the household and the peerage without taking his ministers' advice.

It was during the period of Lord North's ministry, that the tactless handling of the American colonists drove them to armed rebellion, and to the ultimate loss of the colonies, a result for which George III must certainly bear considerable responsibility.

The king was able to control a large number of the members of the Commons by the distribution of bribes, pensions and payment for specially created offices. There was much dissatisfaction at the mismanagement of the war in America, and the people blamed the ministers and the king for choosing them. Members of the Commons were alarmed at the growing power of the king, and a motion that the 'influence of the Crown has increased, is increasing and ought to be diminished' was carried.

In 1782 Lord North resigned, and the new Whig Ministry brought in an Economical Reform Bill to reduce the number of offices and pensions, in order to limit the royal power. The king had lost control of the Commons, but he could

53

still get his way with the Lords. When the Whig government under Fox brought in an India Bill, to take over the government of India by the East India Company and put it under officials who could be appointed by Fox's government, the king sent a message to the Lords saying that whoever voted for the Bill would be considered his enemy. The Bill was thrown out and the Ministry resigned. 'Thank God,' cried the king, 'it is all over, so there is an end to Mr Fox.'

In 1783 William Pitt the Younger, became Prime Minister. He was only twenty-four years old, but the king trusted him, and was anxious not to have to fall back upon one of the Whigs – so for the next seventeen years the king was content to leave the direction of the government to him, especially as his health began to deteriorate. The period of government by the king came to an end, and rule by a trusted and popular Prime Minister took its place.

In 1787 the king went out of his mind. He got out of his carriage one day in Windsor Great Park and addressed an oak tree as the King of Prussia. The next year he recovered, but such an occurrence plainly detracted from the royal power and enhanced that of the Prime Minister. Pitt continued in office until 1801 when he failed to convince the king that the Irish should be granted religious freedom. Pitt resigned.

George IV

The king had repeated spells of madness and in 1811 his disreputable son was appointed Regent. During the next nine years, until the death of his father, the Regent did nothing to sustain the power of the throne, or enhance its reputation. In 1820, he became King George IV. His ten year reign has been described as crammed with little but adulteries, lies and debts. He managed to persuade Parliament to grant him an additional income of £500,000, equivalent to many millions today. He and his brothers wasted vast sums in gambling and drinking. The Duke of Wellington is said to have remarked that the Royal family 'are the damndest millstones about the neck of any government that can be imagined.' The king's only major political activity was to try to prevent Catholic emancipation, but although he caused its postponement, it was ultimately attained in spite of his opposition.

Like his father, George IV was not always quite sane. He had the delusion that he had led a murderous cavalry charge at Waterloo. 'Did I not do so, Arthur?' he would say to the Duke of Wellington. 'I have often heard your Majesty relate the incident' would be the diplomatic reply.

There was no shedding of tears on the death of George IV. On the day of his funeral, *The Times* editorial said 'There never was an individual less regretted by his fellow creatures than the deceased king. What eye has wept for him? What heart has heaved one sob of unmercenary sorrow? . . . If George IV ever had a friend – a devoted friend in any rank of life – we protest that the name of him or her never reached us. An inveterate voluptuary . . . is of all known beings the most selfish. . . .

38 King William IV 'A Respectable old Admiral', Cartoon by George Cruishank

Nothing more remains to be done or said about George IV, but to pay – as pay we must – for his profusion.'

There is no doubt that the Georges had brought widespread and intense unpopularity upon the monarchy. The agitation for Parliamentary reform and an approach to democracy at this time often included a strong anti-royal feeling. Followers of Paine regarded the idea of kingship as sheer tyranny, and Shelley wrote 'Oh that the free would stamp the impious name of king into the dust.' Republicanism and democracy seemed to many people to be inseparably linked. Others argued that if the king had real power to interfere in government, this was anti-democratic; if he had no such power, there was no reason for paying him to do nothing. In either case, monarchy should be abolished.

William IV

William IV did a little to restore the reputation of the monarchy. Although not dissolute like George IV, he was sometimes embarrassingly odd in his behaviour. *The Times* described him as grotesque. On one occasion when a deputation of freemasons came to offer their loyal obedience, he said 'Gentlemen, if my love for you equalled my ignorance of everything about you, it would be boundless.'

On his death in 1837, the *Spectator* wrote 'His late Majesty, though at times a jovial and, for a king, an honest man, was a weak, ignorant, commonplace sort of person. . . . Notwithstanding his feebleness of purpose, and littleness of mind, his ignorance and his prejudice, William IV was to the last a popular sovereign,

55

39 The Reform Act of 1832, Cartoon from *Bell's Weekly Messenger*

but his very popularity was acquired at the price of something like public contempt.'

Since people tended to equate democracy with republicanism it is not surprising that William IV was opposed to Parliamentary reform. Nothing in the world, he declared, would ever induce him to sanction vote by ballot or manhood suffrage. He supported the Lords and their opposition to the Reform Bill of 1831.

A General Election gave Lord Grey, the reforming Prime Minister, an increased majority but the Lords threw out the Bill. Grey resigned, and the king asked the Duke of Wellington to form a government, but he could not get enough support, and Grey once more brought in the Bill. The Lords were opposing the wishes of the people, and there was danger of civil war. Grey advised the king that if necessary, he should create enough new peers to enable the Bill to pass. The king reluctantly agreed. To avoid having the Lords swamped by new Whig peers, the Duke of Wellington advised his followers in the Lords not to vote, and the Bill was carried in 1832.

The king did not like the Whig policies after the Reform Act, and in 1834 dismissed Lord Melbourne, the Prime Minister, and appointed the Tory, Sir Robert Peel. At the election, however, the Whigs still held a majority, and the king was forced to accept Lord Melbourne again. He was furious, and said he would not invite the Whig ministers to dinner. It was clear, however, that no man could be made Prime Minister unless he commanded a majority in the House. No monarch has since then dismissed a Prime Minister.

8 Victoria

Entire and sure the Monarch's rule must prove
Who founds her greatness on her subjects' love.
MATTHEW PRIOR – *Prologue* spoken on Her Majesty's Birthday, 1704

The world is growing weary of that most costly
  of all luxuries, hereditary kings.

GEORGE BANCROFT – letter, 1848

'Ave you 'eard of the Widow at Windsor
With a hairy gold crown on 'er 'ead?
She 'as ships in the foam – she 'as millions at 'ome,
And she pays us poor beggars in red.
Walk wide o' the Widow at Windsor
For 'alf o' creation she owns.
We 'ave bought 'er the same with the sword an' the flame,
An' we've salted it down with our bones.

R. KIPLING, *The Widow at Windsor*

Early Years

After a succession of kings of varying degrees of grotesqueness, debauchery and insanity, the country hoped for better things when the young Princess Victoria came to the throne on the death of William IV in 1837, but there was still a strong republican movement among both middle class radicals and the working class.

40 Coronation of Queen Victoria. The Queen's First Sacrament, from a painting by Leslie

The Chartists assumed that when the working class attained political power the monarchy would vanish together with the House of Lords and other relics of the Middle Ages. Lord Palmerston, the very popular Foreign Secretary, welcomed refugees driven from European countries by autocratic monarchs who were relatives of the queen.

The young queen was intensely serious, and determined to do what she thought best for her people. Her first Prime Minister, Lord Melbourne, was most helpful, but after two years he resigned and Sir Robert Peel formed a Tory government. The Prime Minister claimed the right to make all appointments and asked the queen to dismiss two of her Whig Ladies in Waiting, and replace them with Tories. She indignantly refused, whereupon Peel refused to form a ministry. Melbourne then came back as Prime Minister for another two years, but then he felt that he was too old to continue in office any longer and resigned. Peel once more became Prime Minister, and this time the Queen had to give way to his requests.

The power of the monarch steadily decreased during the nineteenth century, as the political parties became more efficiently organised. Fewer seats were open to royal patronage as elections came to be contested on strictly party lines.

The Queen and the Appointment of the Prime Minister

In 1840 Queen Victoria married her cousin, Prince Albert of Saxe-Coburg. He took a most serious view of the duties of the monarchy, and did much to guide the young queen's actions. Statements such as 'that parliamentary government was on its trial' did not make him popular with English politicians. He studied the English constitution in so far as an unwritten constitution can be accurately studied. In 1852, when Lord Derby had just resigned as Prime Minister, he then advised the Queen to send for Lord Lansdowne as his successor, but Prince Albert interrupted him, telling him that constitutionally he could not give advice and become responsible for it since he was no longer a minister. There was therefore nobody who could properly advise the queen, and she had complete freedom to send for whom she wished.

In practice, of course, her choice was very limited – it would be useless choosing a man who would stand no chance of obtaining sufficient support to form a

41 The State Opening of Parliament by Queen Victoria in 1845. The Queen receives a copy of the Speech from the Lord Chancellor

government. At the present time there is almost always only one possible candidate – the acknowledged leader of the party with a majority in the House of Commons. In 1852, there was no recognised leader, and instead of sending for Lord Lansdowne, the Queen chose Lord Aberdeen.

As time went on this kind of situation arose less frequently. The Queen would still have liked to choose her Prime Ministers. Disraeli, Lord Beaconsfield, flattered her, saying, 'The course of a Ministry depends upon the will of the Queen,' and she was always glad when his Conservative party formed the government. There is no doubt that Disraeli's statement was nearer to the truth during Conservative administrations as the queen herself had little sympathy with the ideas of the Liberals, led by the 'mad radical' Gladstone who, she said, was ruining the country.

In 1880 when the Liberals won a great electoral victory she wrote to her private Secretary, 'What the Queen is especially anxious to have impressed on Lords Hartington and Granville is firstly that Mr Gladstone *she* can have nothing to do with, for she considers his whole conduct since '76 to have been one series of violent passionate invective against and abuse of Lord Beaconsfield. . . . She wishes, however, to support the new Government and to show them confidence, as she has hitherto done all her Governments, but that *this must entirely depend* on their conduct. There must be no democratic leaning, no attempt to change the foreign policy . . . and *no* cutting down of estimates. . . . Mr Lowe she could *not* accept as a minister. Sir C. Dilke she would only and unwillingly consent to having in a *subordinate* office if absolutely necessary.'

The Liberals, however, would not have any leader but Gladstone, so the queen was obliged to accept him. She then tried to obstruct the Liberal leader, both in the selection of ministers and in proposals for legislation. Gladstone, who treated her with unfailing patience had to remind her that scarcely any of her powerful personal friends understood anything about the point of view of the majority of her subjects who had just elected him. On most of the points she had raised the queen failed to get her way, although she insisted upon a letter of apology from Dilke before accepting him as a minister.

In foreign policy she was particularly insistent especially on matters which were affected by Prince Albert's opinions. The prince had been brought up in Europe, and he held strong views on the importance of the monarch's role. The queen wished to give him a constitutional status equal with her own, and even thought of the possibility of making him king, but the government would not even agree to giving him the title of Prince Consort, and in 1841, she used her own prerogative and issued Letters Patent declaring that he should be styled His Royal Highness, with the right to 'have, hold and enjoy pre-eminence and precedence next to herself.'

Prince Albert
Prince Albert was not popular; some people felt that too many Germans had

already wormed their way into English political life. He was not interested in the fashionable pastimes of horse-riding and racing, but preferred science, philosophy and chess. He thought the government should pay more attention to education and housing, but he had no sympathy with the revolutionary refugees from Europe who were welcomed in England both by Palmerston, the Foreign Secretary, and by the working class.

There were attacks upon the prince in the Press, and the queen wrote to the Prime Minister, hoping that the scandalous attacks against the prince 'in several (though none of the *most* respectable) papers would cease' and demanding that the title of Prince Consort should be given him. Even *The Times* referred to difficulties in the prince's constitutional position, and the queen complained that the Government had allowed this '*very* injudicious article' to be printed.

A woman must have a support and an adviser [she wrote] and *who can* this *properly* be but her husband *whose duty it is to watch over her interests private and public.* From this *sacred* duty NO EARTHLY POWER can absolve him! Were it not for the Prince, the Queen's health and strength would long since have sunk under the multifarious duties of her position as Queen and the mother of a large family. Were the Queen to *believe* that these unprincipled and immoral insinuations really were those of *any* but a wicked and despicable few, she would LEAVE a position which nothing but her domestic happiness could make her endure, and retire into private life – leaving the country to choose another ruler after their own HEART'S CONTENT.

Not until 1857 did Victoria obtain the title of Prince Consort for her husband, and then only by her Royal Prerogative.

The prince died in 1861 and everything about his memory was sacred to the queen. She retired almost completely from public life, spending long periods at Balmoral where she insisted on seeing all the State papers, and on receiving personal reports from her ministers.

The Growth of Republicanism

There was growing public discontent at her failure to show herself to the people; and republican sentiment reached a peak about 1870. Many people thought it wrong that the queen should continue to receive large sums of public money every year for which she performed no apparent function.

The fall of Napoleon III and the proclamation of the French Third Republic in September 1870, stimulated republican feeling in Britain. Mass demonstrations were held, and republican clubs formed in most of the large towns. Some members of Parliament were sympathetic, and Charles Bradlaugh published a pamphlet, *An Impeachment of the House of Brunswick* which was widely read. He wrote that Britain would be ready for a republic in a few years, and that it was his 'earnest desire that the present Prince of Wales should never dishonour this country by becoming King.'

Sir Charles Dilke opened a campaign of large public meetings in support of republicanism at one of which Joseph Chamberlain, Mayor of Birmingham presided at the Town Hall. An article in the *Fortnightly Review* said that in the truest sense of the word, Britain was already a republic, though an imperfect one. 'England is now an aristocratic Republic, with a democratic machinery and an hereditary grandmaster of the ceremonies, for a Republic is that State the principle of which is not privilege but merit, where all public power is a free gift and is freely entrusted to those who seem able to use it best.' Monarchy in England, he argued, was therefore a costly but functionless survival.

The Queen and the Constitution

But already the support for republicanism was declining. Disraeli cleverly linked the name of the queen with the new enthusiasm for empire building. The queen was declared the Empress of India, the queen was the head of the world's greatest empire, the queen was made the symbol of Britain's greatness. The ground was prepared for the great burst of royal popularity with which Victoria's reign ended. Meanwhile the queen continued to exert what influence she could over the government of the country.

In 1885 while Gladstone still had a majority, the Queen suggested to Harcourt that a coalition of the Conservatives and some of the Liberals should be formed

43 'New Crowns for Old Ones. The Bill for adding to the Royal Titles that of Empress of India, though pressed forward by the Government, was scarcely approved by the country 1876' From *Punch*, 13 April, 1876

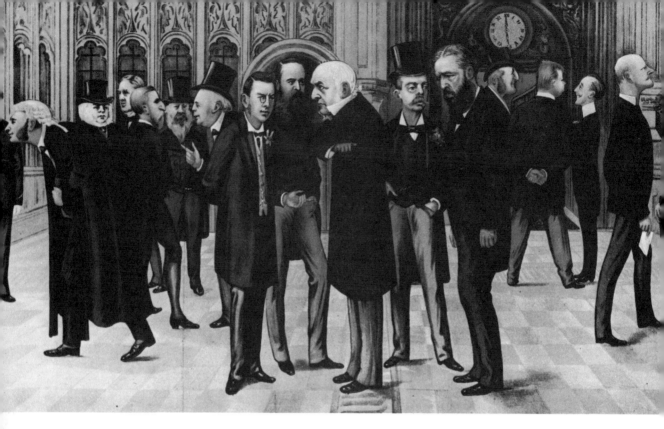

44 The Lobby of the House of Commons in 1886 at the time of the introduction of the Home Rule Bill, with caricatures by 'Ape' of Gladstone, Harcourt, Joseph Chamberlain, Parnell, Randolph Churchill and others

to defeat the Prime Minister whose advice she should constitutionally be asking. Shortly afterwards she wrote to Goschen again suggesting the formation of a 'loyal' National Government in order to defeat the Liberal Party. As Kingsley Martin says in *The Crown and the Establishment*, 'She was a vigorous woman with deep Conservative prejudices; she was the least 'impartial' of mortals and fought against Liberalism bitterly and unscrupulously, taking care only that her opposition should not be public and giving way only when she had no alternative.'

However unconstitutionally Queen Victoria may have acted, she did not seek to overthrow the constitution in any fundamental sense, and although many of her Prime Ministers gave in to some of her frequent and repeated requests, this was usually on matters of lesser importance and her influence in the main course of Britain's history was not great.

The Royal Prerogative

In 1867 Walter Bagehot gave a list of acts which the queen could perform without the consent of Parliament, by the use of the 'Royal Prerogative'. Bagehot wrote, 'The Queen could disband the army, she could dismiss all the officers from the General Commander-in-chief downwards, she could dismiss all the sailors too; she could sell off all our ships of war and all our naval stores; she could make peace by the sacrifice of Cornwall and begin a war for the conquest of Brittany;

she could make every citizen in the United Kingdom, male or female, a peer; she could make every parish in the United Kingdom a university; she could dismiss most of the civil servants; she could pardon all offenders.'

The only safeguard against such actions is the conventional theory that the sovereign can act only on the advice of her ministers. In practice, of course, such actions would require the co-operation of ministers who would almost certainly bring the matter before Parliament, and unless he was prepared to risk Civil War, no sovereign in modern times would contemplate interference of this kind.

The royal powers are today purely formal, and it is understood that the sovereign exercises them only upon the advice of the government. The Crown cannot therefore be held responsible for actions that prove to be foolish or unsuccessful – in other words – 'The King can do no wrong.' As early as 1807, Lord Erskine, after reminding the House of Lords that the sovereign solemnly swears to govern according to the Statues of the realm, and to the laws and customs of the same, said that the maxim that the king can do no wrong 'is not the legal fiction of the constitution, but the practical benefit and blessing of it,' for it preserves the untarnished image of royalty, while guaranteeing the real power of Parliament.

Queen Victoria did use the Royal Prerogative when by Sign Manual she abolished the practice of officers purchasing their commissions in the army. This

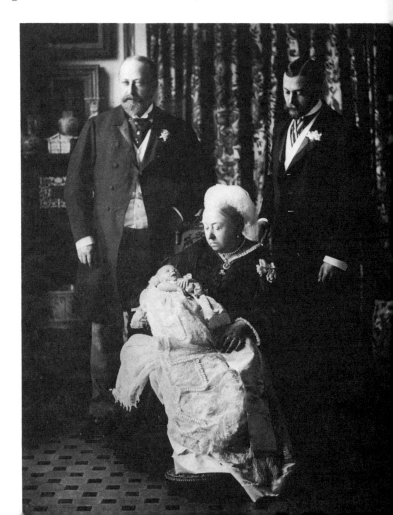

45 Queen Victoria nursing the future King Edward VIII at his christening in 1894. With her are the future Kings Edward VII and George V

was to enable the government to overcome the opposition of the Lords to a measure which the government felt was necessary.

This practice has frequently been used when rapid legislation has been needed, and the government has wished to avoid the delays and complication of a normal Parliamentary Bill. The Royal Prerogative, in the form of Orders in Council, Signs Manual and Warrants is thus useful to the government.

The Prestige of the Queen

The general public knew little of Queen Victoria's behind-the-scenes political activities, thanks largely to the patience and reticence of Gladstone and her other ministers. To the people, she was the best sovereign Britain had had for centuries. After the extravagancies, and immorality of most of the Hanoverians before her, Victoria was a model of rectitude. Her family life was blameless, her religious observance exemplary, her carriage royal and dignified. Instead of being feared, loathed or despised, the monarchy became an object of love, respect and admiration. By the time of her Golden Jubilee great crowds cheered her progress through London.

There was still considerable feeling against the queen, and against the idea of royalty generally, however. On 19 July, 1887, just before the Jubilee, *Reynolds Newspaper* said 'Will any flunky in Christendom tell us one good thing that the Queen, her sons and daughters, or any one of her inexhaustible brood of pauper relations "made in Germany" has ever done for the people of this land? . . . But the injuries inflicted on the masses have alas been serious indeed. The robbery and the jobbery, of which the Queen has been the "heart and soul" are simply appalling. . . . In fifty years she has wrung from them directly and indirectly from eighty to ninety millions sterling. She has jobbed all her children and German cousins into the highest public offices without the slightest regard to their qualifications, or rather positive disqualifications. . . .

At Westminster Abbey next Tuesday, ten thousand persons . . . all blasphemously falling down and worshipping a pampered old woman of sullen visage and sordid mind, because she is supposed to have in her veins some of the tainted fluid which coursed in those of that devotee of Sodom and Gomorrah, James I! Think of it, just Heavens!'

This is a point of view not given much publicity today, but it was certainly held in the nineteenth century, perhaps with some reason.

Victoria's Diamond Jubilee was evidence of greater loyalty. The queen had gradually come to be a sort of ideal figure – the perfect mother, the perfect lady. To many people whose lives were drab, the royal family brought a vicarious splendour. At the same time, the queen had become a symbol of the greatness of Britain and the British Empire, so the wave of jingoistic patriotism became also a glorification of the monarchy. As Compton Mackenzie wrote – 'her Diamond Jubilee almost made the public believe that she personally during her long reign had created the British Empire.'

46 *Above:* Queen Victoria's Diamond Jubilee. The Queen leaving Buckingham Palace

47 *Below:* Queen Victoria's Diamond Jubilee. The Queen in her carriage at St. Paul's Cathedral for the thanksgiving service

By the time of her death, Victoria had set the pattern of royalty for the new century – kindly, gracious and a pillar of the Church and the Constitution. During the last few years of her reign, she was able to influence the conduct of government less and less, as the party system became more highly organised, but the more she withdrew from government, the more deeply she was revered, and the more closely she became identified with the people. Edward VII had no easy task adequately to follow such a paragon.

48 King Edward VII when Prince of Wales, visiting Queen Victoria. Caricature by Max Beerbohm, 1921. 'The rare and rather awful visits of Albert Edward, Prince of Wales, to Windsor Castle.'

9 Edward VII and George V

Whoever is king, is also the father of his country.
                    CONGREVE, *Love for Love.*

Not making his high place the lawless perch
Of wing'd ambitions, nor a vantage ground
For pleasure; but thro' all this tract of years
Wearing the white flower of a blameless life
Before a thousand peering littlenesses.
                    TENNYSON, *Idylls of the King.*

A Constitutional King

Prince Edward had always been a bitter disappointment to Queen Victoria. He had received a very strict upbringing. His father was most anxious that he should be educated as befitted a prince and heir to the throne; no time could be spared for sport and recreation; it was books and study, morning, afternoon and evening. But it was all to no avail – books never had much attraction for him.

On his seventeenth birthday, his father presented him with a lengthy document which began 'Life is composed of duties.' But duty had no more attraction for Prince Edward than books. As soon as he passed from his father's jurisdiction, he reacted violently against his upbringing, and devoted his life to a perpetual round of pleasures – and the pleasures which were least acceptable to the queen. She did not like his friends, and when they led him into bacarat scandals and the divorce court, her righteous indignation would have crushed anyone but Prince Edward. Every year, she gave him a lecture upon the evils of horse-racing.

By the time of his mother's death, however, he was in his sixtieth year, and had long sown his wild oats. For a long time he had asked the queen to allow him to share in government affairs, but she refused, saying it would be unconstitutional for him to know secrets of state – in any case, considering the sort of people he associated with, it would be dangerous. Edward VII was therefore not very well prepared for the position of monarch.

He was anxious not to contravene the Constitution. He showed none of his mother's dislike of the Liberal Party, and made no attempt to choose or exclude any particular politician. He had travelled extensively, and had considerable knowledge of foreign affairs, but he was generally content to act in accordance with ministerial advice. He thus completed the pattern of royalty for the twentieth century, giving not only the appearance, but the reality of complete respect for the Constitution. He increased the social position of his Prime Ministers by giving them precedence over most other persons at dinner parties, and other social functions.

On one constitutional point Edward VII had a difference of opinion with his Prime Minister, and this concerned foreign affairs. He had many friends in France, and this had helped the British and French governments to come to the agreement of the Entente Cordiale. The Bill ratifying this contained a reference to a small cession of territory. The king maintained that cession of territory was a Royal Prerogative, and did not need the approval of Parliament. Mr Balfour insisted that Parliament must have the opportunity to accept or reject the proposal. The king was obliged to give way.

The king also felt justified in visiting foreign sovereigns, and discussing problems with them, without being accompanied by any minister of the Crown. He was always careful to inform his ministers what had been said on these visits, but some members of the cabinet thought a minister should always be present at such interviews.

Edward VII added an important and popular element to the image of royalty, he greatly increased the pageantry of royal occasions, and so gave the crowds some splendid spectacles which appealed to the general public. He revived the old custom of opening Parliament in person.

George V 1910–1936

Constitutional Problems: The House of Lords   George V reigned during a time of crises, both national and international. The first one was already under way before the death of Edward VII. The Liberal government had introduced a budget which Lloyd George, the Chancellor said was meant to 'take money from the rich in order to help the poor'. It was overwhelmingly passed by the Commons, but so angry were the Lords at this 'confiscation of wealth' as they called it, that they broke what had for a long time been considered a part of the Constitution, they threw out a money Bill.

Asquith, the Prime Minister, declared that this was a 'breach of the Constitution, and a usurpation of the rights of the Commons'. A general election

49 Four Monarchs: King Edward VII and the future Kings George V, Edward VIII and George VI

followed in which the Liberals asked the electorate to empower them to curb the power of the Lords. Asquith declared that the Liberals would not again take office unless the king assured him that he would create enough new peers to ensure the passing of the budget. The king's private secretary wrote to inform Asquith that the king 'regards the policy of the Government as tantamount to the destruction of the House of Lords, and he thinks that before a large creation of peers is embarked upon or threatened, the country should be acquainted with the particular project for accomplishing such destruction.'

Lord Esher, one of the king's unofficial advisers urged the king to refuse to create peers before the general election. If the government resigned because of such a refusal, he said, the king would be supported by the country, and all over Europe. In a letter to his son, Lord Esher said 'If the king says "Yes", he mortally offends the whole Tory Party to which he is naturally bound. If he says no, he lets loose all the Radical gutter Press at his position as sovereign and his person as a man. A charming dilemma, full of revolutionary possibilities. We have never been nearer to revolution since 1688.'

At the election the Liberals were returned again with a majority of only two over the Conservatives, but they could count on the support of the Labour and Irish members. The budget was again presented, and this time the Lords passed it without a division.

A few days later King Edward died, and no sooner had George V become king than the constitutional battle was resumed with even more intensity. The Liberals introduced the Parliament Bill, to deprive the Lords of all power to reject a money Bill, and to reduce their power in regard to other Bills to delaying them, but ensuring that if passed by the Commons in three successive sessions, all Bills would become law in spite of rejection by the Lords. The Bill passed the Commons, but was rejected by the Lords, and Asquith asked for a dissolution of Parliament so that the people could express their opinion.

Asquith told the king that he might have to ask him to create enough new peers to overcome the Lords' resistance. Since the Conservatives were wholly in support of the Lords' point of view, the king was placed in a difficult position. It had long been the view that the sovereign was above party politics, and that he should not identify himself with one party against the other. The Conservatives argued that the Prime Minister had no right to extract a promise from the king as to what he would do if the Liberals were returned to power at the forthcoming election.

The king, with Asquith's agreement, discussed the matter with the opposition leaders, on the understanding that there was a distinction between 'desiring knowledge' from the Opposition, and 'seeking advice' from the Prime Minister. The king was most anxious to act constitutionally. At the election the Liberals would claim that they, on behalf of the people, were challenging the right of the Lords to baulk the will of the people. Could the king allow the Conservatives to use his name to defeat the will of the people? The king made it clear that he would follow the Premier's advice and 'most reluctantly' he gave Asquith a secret

69

understanding that he would create the new peers if necessary. The Liberals were successful in this second election in 1910, and the king's undertaking was then read to the Lords, and they accepted the Parliament Bill.

Ireland No sooner had this crisis passed than another arose. The Liberal Government introduced a Home Rule Bill for Ireland, which would set up a Parliament at Dublin to deal with purely Irish affairs. There was intense opposition in Ulster, where the Protestants, who formed a majority there, were unwilling to be subjected to the rule of Ireland's Catholic majority.

The Bill was passed by the Commons in the face of determined Conservative opposition, and rejected by the Lords, introduced a second time and passed by the Commons and again rejected. It was again passed by the Commons in 1914. The Lords could delay it no longer, and the Protestants of Ulster declared that they would rebel, rather than accept the Act. Conservative leaders backed the Ulstermen, and the king was given some very dubious advice. Some argued that the normal constitutional rules did not apply to changes in the structure of the empire, and Lord Esher said it was the king's duty to dismiss Parliament although the Government had a large majority. Other Conservative leaders maintained that the king still had the right to veto any Act of Parliament. Some officers of the army declared that they would refuse to move against the Ulstermen if they rebelled, saying that they were willing to promote civil war, and to obey the personal wishes of the king against those of his government.

The king was very worried. Some of the Ulstermen and their Conservative supporters were his personal friends. He felt that his oath as a Protestant ruler made it questionable whether it was right to give rule to the Catholic Irish. He was troubled at the thought of civil war. He suggested to Asquith that a general election would clear the air, and show whether the government really had a mandate for Home Rule. He even said he might 'feel it his duty to do what in his own judgment was best for the people generally'.

Asquith reminded the king that the veto had not been used for over two hundred years, and was now as dead as Queen Anne, and that it was unconstitutional to reject the advice of a Prime Minister who still commanded a majority in the Commons.

In May, the King felt that he must take the initiative. He asked the Speaker of the House of Commons if he would preside at a conference. He then asked the Prime Minister to arrange one, and on 17 July, Mr Asquith agreed that 'a conference be held under Your Majesty's auspices at Buckingham Palace for a free and full discussion of the outstanding issues.' The conference met on the 21 July but was unable to come to a satisfactory conclusion.

The king was relieved of the responsibility of making a final decision by the outbreak of the First World War, when the Home Rule Bill was shelved.

Although George V on all major matters accepted the advice of his Prime Ministers, he sometimes used his right to protest and warn. When the government was introducing a Bill to deal with the suffragettes who were going on hunger strike while in prison, the King's secretary wrote – 'His Majesty cannot help feeling that there is something shocking, if not almost cruel in the operation to which these insensate women are subjected through their refusal to take necessary nourishment. . . . The King asks whether in your "Temporary Discharge of Prisons Bill" it would not be possible to abolish forcible feeding.'

When the Irish question arose again after the war, and British Government troops were taking reprisals against the Irish people, the king repeatedly wrote to his ministers asking what the government 'intended to do towards further protecting the lives of unoffending people in Ireland.' 'The King,' said Sir Harold Nicolson 'regarded himself – it was an honourable illusion – as the protector of his Irish as well as his British subjects.'

George V also maintained his right in some cases to refuse the Premier's wishes in the awarding of honours. In at least one case, when Lloyd George wished to sell a peerage to a millionaire, the king objected, and refused to give way. Usually, however, the king expostulated, but ultimately gave his reluctant approval.

The Crown and the Establishment   The king had also another source of influence over the conduct of affairs. He stands at the head of what is known as the Establishment. Besides the members of the Royal Family, and their connections, there are the private secretaries, the great aristocratic families, the archbishops and senior bishops, who have been appointed by the Crown, the Governor of the Bank of England and his colleagues, senior civil servants, the service chiefs, the intelligence and secret service officers. If not already members of the Establishment, Prime Ministers and their senior colleagues are almost inevitably incorporated in it though sometimes accepted somewhat on sufferance; while the Leader of the Opposition is paid a substantial salary and usually feels that he too is part of this anomalous but powerful body.

The monarch has contacts with all sections of the Establishment, and can do much to hold it together, guide the climate of opinion, and influence appointments to important positions. Lord Esher was one of the pillars of the Establishment for many years. Each volume of his journals and letters begins with the following quotation from Lord Beaconsfield – 'The most powerful men are not public men. The public man is responsible, and the responsible man is a slave. It is private life that governs the world.'

The story of Sir Douglas Haig reveals how strong the influence of the king and the Establishment could be in opposing the wishes of the Prime Minister. Haig, who had married one of the queen's maids of honour, was a personal friend of both King Edward VII and George V. He was Commander-in-Chief at Aldershot when the war broke out.

The army chiefs believed that the only way to win the war was to batter on at the Western Front irrespective of losses, until at last the greater Allied resources of manpower would leave those of the enemy so depleted that victory would be

certain and in the words of Kingsley Martin, 'they believed, against all the evidence, in their own unique competence'. Some of the politicians, particularly Lloyd George and Churchill were horrified at the callous attitude of the High Command to the appalling loss of life entailed in this 'war of attrition', and their refusal to consider alternative strategies.

Haig was able to persuade the king of the rightness of his approach, and of his own competence. 'The King,' he wrote 'will support me "through thick and thin", but I must be careful not to resign, because Lloyd George would then appeal to the country for support, and would probably come back with a great majority.'

Thus, the High Command, with the backing of the king tried to circumvent the elected government. Neither side in this struggle was over-scrupulous. Lloyd George made a secret agreement with the French Commander-in-Chief by which Haig found himself subordinate to the French General. To substantiate their claim, the British generals minimised British casualty figures and exaggerated those of the Germans.

The king admired Haig's tenacity and his 'rock-like calm' in the face of his dismal, disastrous failures. The king said the politicians must not interfere with the strategy of the army leaders. It is probable that the king was not informed of the dangerous state of morale in the French army which was mutinous in 1917, while the appalling losses were having an adverse effect upon the spirit of the British forces.

In February 1918 Lloyd George managed to get rid of Sir William Robertson, CIGS, and Haig's most influential supporter. The king's secretary wrote to Robertson, begging him not to relinquish the post, but Lloyd George was adamant – if the king insisted on Robertson remaining in office, the Government would resign. The king gave way: the Government triumphed over an attempt at military dictation backed by the king – but only partially. Sir Douglas Haig remained Commander-in-Chief to the end of the war. Early in November 1918, as the war was rapidly approaching its end, Lloyd George asked the king to dissolve

Parliament which had now been sitting for eight years. The king was very reluctant, and suggested several reasons why he thought an election should be postponed. The Prime Minister, however, countered the king's arguments with others and insisted upon a dissolution. The king felt obliged to agree. Had he not done so, Lloyd George would have resigned, and if, as appeared probable, no one else would have been willing or able to form a government, the king would have been forced to call upon Lloyd George to form a caretaker Government, and then grant a dissolution.

The King and the Labour Governments   The king's anxiety that the smooth running of the Establishment should not be upset by an unsympathetic government was aroused in 1924 by the possibility of a Labour Government. He was relieved to find that the Labour Prime Minister was no revolutionary, and that he appointed an Establishment man in charge of defence. The king was very affable, and the Government, which was dependent upon the Liberals for support, was not tempted to introduce any very left wing proposals.

The Labour Government was defeated in October 1924, and the Prime Minister asked for a dissolution. The king did not wish to plunge the country into another general election less than a year after the previous one, and since the Prime Minister did not command a majority in the Commons, he was not under a constitutional obligation to grant a dissolution. He enquired whether the leader of either the Liberal or the Conservative Party would form a government, or join a coalition government. Neither leader was willing, so the king was obliged to grant the dissolution.

In 1931, the Second Labour Government presented the king with a problem. There was a financial crisis, and the Cabinet were divided. Ramsay MacDonald, the Prime Minister, informed the king that some of his colleagues in the cabinet intended to resign, and that he would be unable to carry on the government, so he offered his resignation. The king felt that the situation was critical, and it would be unwise to increase the state of anxiety in the nation by having a general election. He therefore approached the leaders of the Conservative and Liberal Parties and suggested that they should form a coalition government. Sir Herbert Samuel, the Liberal leader thought that the people would most readily accept the proposed economies from a National Government, with a Labour Prime Minister, and he expressed his willingness to serve under Mr MacDonald. Mr Baldwin, the Conservative leader was also willing, and all three leaders agreed to form a National Government on condition that the king would grant a dissolution as soon as Britain's credit had been strengthened. The king had undoubtedly done what he thought was best in what seemed to be a national emergency. The Liberal and Conservative Party leaders thought that the king had acted quite constitutionally, but many Labour supporters felt that he had been encouraged into an unpleasant political manoeuvre by Mr MacDonald, which had done great harm to the Labour Party.

The King and the Choice of Prime Minister   King George V had a rather different but equally difficult problem in 1923 when he was called upon to make a definite choice of Prime Minister. It was one which fell within the ranks of the Establishment. Mr Bonar Law, the Prime Minister, was dangerously ill – too ill to advise the king as to his successor, and there were two possible claimants – Lord Curzon, a senior leader of the Conservative Party, a very experienced Cabinet Minister and a life-long friend of the king – and Stanley Baldwin, Chancellor of the Exchequer, but much less well known. It was generally expected that the king would choose Lord Curzon; but he was a peer, while Baldwin was a commoner, and the king had to consider what would be the effect of choosing a Prime Minister who was in the Lords. It would probably be considered as undemocratic. The Liberals would object that they would have no means of questioning him. The Labour Party would be even more dissatisfied. They were a growing force and might before long form a government; it was important that the king should not appear to be hostile to the Labour Party. The king asked the advice of Mr Balfour, an elder statesman of the Conservative Party, a former Prime Minister. He said that 'In the present state of politics, the Prime Minister ought to be in the House of Commons.' The king then decided that it must be Mr Baldwin, and he informed Lord Curzon that he felt that he must ignore the personal element, and that he believed he would not be fulfilling his trust were he now to make his selection of Prime Minister from the House of Lords.

The King as the Symbol of the Nation   It has been said that George V set the tone of the monarchy for the twentieth century. He was correct in all matters, con-

51   The Commonwealth. The Queen standing with two ministers and seven premiers of seven countries of the Commonwealth

servative, drawing his friends from the traditional landowning aristocracy. He was meticulous in carrying out his duties, and obviously sincere. As head of the army, he paid frequent visits to the front in the First World War. As head of the Church, he upheld the Protestant religion, but he refused to sign the Protestant Declaration at his coronation as he felt that it contained passages which would be offensive to his Roman Catholic subjects. He merely swore that he was a faithful Protestant.

In 1931, the Statute of Westminster defined the position of the king with regard to the Empire, which was now called the Commonwealth. The Dominions were recognised as independent, equal states, but they were united by a common allegiance to the Crown. In future 'any alteration in the law touching the Succession to the Throne or the Royal State and Titles shall hereafter require the assent as well of the Parliaments of all the Dominions as of the Parliament of the United Kingdom.'

The following year the king began the custom of broadcasting a Christmas message to the Commonwealth. It was a tremendous success; he was speaking to all the people, over the heads of the politicians and the courtiers. He became a human being, speaking to them in their own homes – 'I am speaking,' he said, 'to the children above all. Remember, children, the King is speaking to you.'

George V managed to combine the image of the monarch, aloof, above politics, the head of a world-wide commonwealth, with that of a simple, affectionate family man. His eldest son, Edward, said of him, 'My father, with the instinctive genius of a simple man, found the means of squaring the apparent circle within the resources of his own character. By the force of his own authentic example – the King himself in the role of the bearded *paterfamilias*, his devoted and queenly wife, their four grown sons and a daughter, not to mention the rising generation of grandchildren – he transformed the crown as personified by the Royal Family, into a model of the traditional family virtues. . . . The King, as the dutiful father, became the living symbol not only of the nation, but also of the Empire, the last link holding together these diversified and scattered communities.' (from *A King's Story*).

George V's stern sense of duty did not endear him to his sons. When Lord Derby suggested that he might cultivate the friendship of his sons, he replied, 'My father was frightened of his mother: I was frightened of my father, and I am damned well going to see to it that my children are frightened of me.' His son Edward reacted against his father's ideas – he seems to have been born something of a rebel.

10 Edward VIII and George VI

What infinite heart's ease
Must kings neglect, that private men enjoy!
And what have kings, that privates have not too
Save ceremony, save general ceremony?

SHAKESPEARE, *Henry V.*

To be a kingdom's bulwark, a king's glory
Yet loved by both, and trusted and trustworthy
Is more than to be king.

COLERIDGE 'Zapolya'.

The clearest mark of a true king is that he
is one whom all good men can praise without
compunction not only during his life but even
afterwards.

DEO CHRYSOSTOM, *First Discourse on Kingship.*

Edward VIII

Edward became king in 1936 with few of the characteristics of his father. He was a bachelor, he did not care for the ritual of royalty, he chose his friends from different circles, but he took his duties as king very seriously. What changes he might have tried to introduce we do not know, for a crisis arose almost immediately. He was in love with an American lady who had already been divorced, and he wished to marry her. Mr Baldwin, the Prime Minister and the Archbishop of Canterbury, agreed that such a marriage, in view of the Church's doctrine on divorce, would be a very bad example to the country. The king felt that he could not perform his duties as king without being with the woman he loved, and that if this could not be arranged, it would be his duty to abdicate. Had he been one of the earlier Hanoverians, there would have been no problem – he would have lived with her as his mistress, but times had changed: his grandmother and father had created a very different image of the British monarchy.

A few people including Mr Winston Churchill, tried to persuade the king to marry as he wished, and to refuse to abdicate. He had no wish to form a king's party, and split the nation: such a course could only damage the monarchy, so he was loyal to his oath and took the Prime Minister's advice and gave up the throne. His brother George became King George VI.

George VI and his Prime Ministers

George V's second son reacted very differently to his father's system of education. He was a slow, timid boy, and took to heart his father's frequent rebukes. The boys

52 The Abdication of King Edward VIII. A Demonstration at Marble Arch in his favour

were not sent to school, but had a private tutor, who reported regularly on his pupils' conduct and progress, or lack of it. Then came the summons to the library, and the interview with the stern father. In the end, George modelled himself as closely as possible upon his father, and so the tradition of monarchy established by Victoria was continued.

George VI, as the younger, less gifted brother, neither expected nor desired to be king. He did not like publicity, and had looked forward to the quiet life of a country gentleman; but he had a strong sense of duty, and in spite of his nervous stammer, he forced himself to perform his public duties, and overcome the disability and broadcast to the Commonwealth. He was really well suited to the routine of court life: he was naturally conservative and while he would have liked to improve working-class conditions, he was afraid of fundamental change. He never allowed his personal feelings to interfere with his strictly constitutional duties, but he used his right to discuss matters with his Prime Ministers, and frequently warned Mr Attlee that the Labour Government was introducing changes with dangerous speed, and threatening the liberty of the subject: however, he accepted Attlee's long explanations and assurances.

He was most emphatic in his opposition to the granting of independence to India, maintaining that 'India must be governed', and that to release Gandhi from jail would be suicidal. In the end, however, he accepted the Prime Minister's advice, as the constitution required, and India gained its independence.

The king was most anxious that the right man should be appointed as Prime Minister. He had to choose in 1940 when Neville Chamberlain lost the confidence of the House, including many of his own party. The king admired Chamberlain,

53 The King and Queen in London during the bombing

and offered to try to persuade Mr Attlee to serve under him, but Mr Chamberlain was unwilling. The leaders of all parties agreed that there must be a National Government, but the Labour leaders said they would not serve under Mr Chamberlain. It was clear, therefore, that there must be a new Prime Minister. The king had a choice between two men: Lord Halifax and Winston Churchill. Mr Chamberlain discussed the matter with them as to which of them he should recommend to the king. He himself would have preferred his old friend and colleague, Lord Halifax, but they had to bear in mind the attitude of the Labour Party who were opposed to the idea of a Prime Minister in the Lords. Lord Halifax said he thought it would be very difficult for him to discharge the duties of Prime Minister and it became clear to Chamberlain that he would have to recommend Churchill. The king said he would prefer Lord Halifax, and suggested that some arrangement might be made to enable Halifax to answer questions in the Commons, but when Chamberlain said that this would lead to bitter opposition, he reluctantly agreed to send for Mr Churchill.

Mr Churchill as Prime Minister, made many journeys during the war, and there was the danger that he might meet his death. The king was anxious to do the right thing, if that should occur, and wished to avoid having to make another difficult choice. He therefore asked Mr Churchill to suggest whom his successor should be if he should be killed on active service. Mr Churchill named Mr Eden, the leading personality in the Conservative Party, which was the largest party in the Commons. It was therefore reasonable to assume that he would command a majority in the House. Fortunately the need to follow this advice did not arise.

The King and the Dissolution of Parliament

One of the Prime Minister's most valuable rights is that of deciding when to ask for a dissolution, and so choose the time for a General Election. In the election of February 1950, the Labour Party were returned to office with the narrow majority of eight. The king thought that this did not give the government a mandate to enact very socialistic policies. He feared that the government might soon be defeated and this would mean a request for another general election. He was doubtful whether he ought to comply with a request for dissolution. It was suggested that it would be better to form a coalition government than to have an election. Mr Churchill, Leader of the Conservative Opposition thought the Labour Government had a constitutional right to continue in office 'until some fresh issue or situation has arisen to place before the electorate'. The Government agreed, and continued in office for eighteen months.

The king continued to be anxious; he would have liked a more settled House of Commons, with a government which could depend upon a fairly substantial majority. He was due to go on a tour of the Commonwealth in the autumn of 1951, and he wished to leave the country in a settled state. He again approached Mr Attlee, who then agreed to ask for a dissolution in the first week of October, but to what extent he was influenced by the king, and to what extent he decided that this would be a good time from the point of view of the Labour Party, is not known.

George VI was concerned for the welfare of his people in a paternalistic way. As Duke of York he had started an annual camp where equal numbers of public schoolboys and youths working in mines and factories, lived together for a fortnight. He did not, however, wish in any way to undermine the position of the upper classes or the Establishment.

During the war, the king and queen continued to live in the palace throughout the bombing of London, sharing the dangers of the people. Their example was a great encouragement and inspired people of different classes to work together to give mutual support against enemy action. Loyalty and affection for the royal family increased.

11 Queen Elizabeth II

She had all the royal makings of a queen
As holy oil, Edward Confessor's crown,
The rod, and bird of peace, and all such emblems
Laid nobly on her.

SHAKESPEARE, *Henry VIII.*

The Queen and Court Procedure

In 1953, King George VI died, and once more Britain had a young queen. Some people hoped that the 'wind of change' which was blowing over so much of the modern world and particularly in much of the British Commonwealth, would sweep away some of the rigidity of court procedure, and bring the monarchical pattern more into tune with the post-war world. Little happened, however, for it was generally felt in the Establishment, that the monarchy enshrines the great traditions of the country, and that it must continue to keep up the appearance of those traditions, in order to retain their reality. How far these traditions are vital for the prosperity of the nation today, or how far they are a handicap is a matter of opinion. There seems little doubt that the queen's sympathies are with the Establishment. Paul Johnson wrote in 1969, 'So far as we can judge, Queen Elizabeth has conformed strictly to the constitutional practices laid down by Edward VII, and to the social attitudes of her father and grandfather. She made a "suitable" marriage, and has encouraged other members of her family to do likewise; she is strictly conformist in religion, and interests herself in the doings of the clergy; she performs her role as head of the Commonwealth with great assiduity; she reads her official papers carefully and is polite to her ministers, whatever their political colour; she goes through the democratic motions and entertains a wide variety of her subjects at informal lunch parties; but she selects her private friends from exactly the same circle as George VI; she shoots birds in Norfolk and stalks deer in Scotland; she ardently upholds the traditional royal patronage of the turf and bloodstock; and in her public utterances she confines herself to the plain diet of clichés, and platitudes prepared by the royal secretariat.'

The Coronation

Nevertheless, vast numbers of people are quite happy with the monarchy as it is. Huge crowds line the streets to witness ceremonies such as the Coronation, and still larger numbers see them on television. To some, they are just gorgeous pageants, to be enjoyed for their colour and pageantry, but to others they epitomise the long story of British development, and the even longer history of monarchy itself.

The Coronation service is substantially the same as that of King Edgar at Bath in AD 973, and in it are elements recalling the Teutonic, Christian and Norman-French strands of our nation.

There is a hint of the magic of prehistoric kingship in the 'Stone of Destiny' on which the kings of Scotland had been crowned, and which was stolen by King Edward I and brought to England. It is now placed beneath the Coronation Chair. The significance of the Coronation ceremony cannot be better described than by quoting from Harold Nicolson's book on *The Monarchy*:

> The element of magic is also reflected in the extraordinary ritual of the Coronation service. The Queen is acclaimed with all the pomp of a great temporal sovereign; she is at the same time dedicated, almost as a sacrificial victim, to the service of her God and her peoples. There she sits clad in a tunic of cloth of gold, solitary and humble, modest and majestic, aloof and detached. . . .
>
> The king-priest element is also suggested by the service. The Queen is dressed in sacerdotal robes, in cope and stole; she moves slowly backwards and forwards across the theatre to the sound of anthems and the shouts of welcoming acolytes; she holds a Bible in her hand. The Church proclaims her its servant and she kneels humbly to the ministrations of the Church. The ritual is predominantly ecclesiastical; . . .
>
> The king-warrior element is symbolised by the great swords that are delivered

55 The Coronation of Queen Elizabeth II. The Supreme Moment: the Queen sits in St. Edward's chair wearing St. Edward's crown, after it had been placed on her head by the Archbishop of Canterbury

to her and carried naked before her in the processions. Menacing and splendid the swords flash as they move down the aisle, and among them is 'Curtana', the sword of Mercy, with its point stubbed and snapped.

The old Teutonic system of election is symbolised by the Recognition with which the service begins. The Queen is presented to the congregation and is acclaimed, not as was the old custom by the knights clashing their swords upon their shields, but by the boys of Westminster School shouting, '*Vivat Regina Elizabetha! Vivat! Vivat! Vivat!*', in sturdy unison. The helmet with which the tribal leaders were crowned in Teutonic days has been replaced by a crown of velvet, fur, gold and jewels.

The anointing, which is regarded by the Church as the supreme ceremony of the Coronation, implies that, even as Zadok the priest and Nathan the prophet anointed Solomon, so also are the monarchs of England anointed by the heads of the Church. From the ampulla the Dean of Westminster pours a few drops of oil into the spoon which he hands to the Archbishop. The Archbishop then anoints the Queen upon her head, her hands and her breast. From then on the Queen becomes 'the Lord's anointed': her person is holy.

The Coronation ends with the purely feudal rite of homage. The dukes, the earls, the barons kneel before her, promising to become her 'Liege man of Life and Limb and of earthly worship'.

The Proclamation of the Accession is signed by Privy Councillors, the Lord Mayor and Alderman and by 'other gentlemen of quality'. The service opens with the Recognition ceremony, a reminder that the succession in Anglo-Saxon times was partially elective. The Archbishop advances towards each of the four corners of the abbey in turn, saying – 'Sirs, I here present unto you Queen Elizabeth your undoubted Queen. Wherefore, all ye who are come this day to do your homage and service, are ye willing to do the same?' The trumpets sound, and the boys of Westminster School shout four times 'God Save Queen Elizabeth!'

The Archbishop then administers the oath, and the queen promises to govern according to the laws and customs of her different peoples, and to 'cause Law and Justice in Mercy' to be executed in her judgments. She then promises to maintain the Protestant Reformed religion established by law.

After communion comes the ceremony of the anointing, and then the queen is robed, and presented with the spurs, the sword, bracelets, Stole Royal and other symbolic regalia.

Then the queen is crowned, the choirboys shout 'God Save the Queen,' the trumpets sound and the guns at the Tower of London thunder a salute. The Archbishop of Canterbury now performs the Act of Homage on behalf of the Church, followed by the Duke of Edinburgh who says, 'I, Philip, Duke of Edinburgh become your liege man of life and limb and of earthly worship.' The queen changes crowns and robes, and slowly leaves the Abbey for her golden coach, and the cheering crowds.

There are several reasons why the Coronation ceremony has been retained, as well as the English love of tradition for its own sake. It reinforces the prestige of the Reformed Church and it reaffirms the rights of the nobles under Magna Carta contained in the Coronation Oath. The members of the House of Commons take no part whatever in the ceremony, being herded together in an upper gallery; but as the power of government lies in their hands, they can afford to leave the show and pageant to the monarch and the Lords.

Many people who feel that the monarchy has an important and useful part to play in modern Britain, regretted that the Coronation ceremony was so steeped

56 The Coronation of Queen Elizabeth II. The Queen, holding the Royal Sceptre, ensign of kingly power and justice, and the Rod with the Dove, Rod of equity and mercy, prepares to receive homage

in medievalism, and couched in almost incomprehensible feudal jargon. The country had been told that the monarchy symbolised our increasingly democratic way of life, and that the coronation would help to unite the nation, but all the participants were from the aristocracy and the Establishment (not even any member of the House of Commons, and certainly no representative of the working class). There was no indication that the vast majority of the queen's subjects were not Christians, but Hindus, Buddhists and Moslems. As Kingsley Martin said, 'the ceremony was more purely national, more aristocratic, more exclusive, more Anglican, more medieval than ever before.' And yet the people seemed to enjoy it thoroughly. There is no doubt that the monarchy is still highly popular.

The popularity of the British royal family extends far beyond Britain and the Commonwealth; in fact many of the newspapers on the continent of Europe and in the USA seem to display more interest in their activities than does the British press.

This interest has become a valuable economic asset, as the ceremonies connected with the reigning monarch, and the buildings and regalia associated with past kings and queens form one of the chief tourist attractions which bring millions of foreign visitors to Britain, and the hundreds of millions of pounds worth of various foreign currencies which they spend here.

Besides the pageantry of the occasional ceremonies such as the coronation, there are the routine activities such as the changing of the Guard which always attract a little crowd of foreign visitors.

One of the most colourful and important state ceremonies is the opening of Parliament by the monarch. That in which Queen Elizabeth II opens a Parliament in the 1970s is almost exactly similar in outward form to that of Elizabeth I four hundred years ago; but the reality behind it is very different.

The ceremony takes place in what is termed 'her own' Palace of Westminster, but which is really the Houses of Parliament. There, preceded by her heralds, magnificently apparelled, and wearing the royal crown, the Queen takes her place on the throne. Before her sit the twenty-six Lords Spiritual, representing the Church of England, and hundreds of Lords Temporal, all robed in ermine and velvet. But there are no members of the House of Commons. Then an official messenger named Black Rod is sent to summon the Commons to the Upper House.

Black Rod passes through the long corridor to the door of the House of Commons, but it is slammed in his face. Then a little wicket is opened, and he is asked his business. He states that he brings a message from the queen, and he is admitted. He then delivers his message, and summons the Commons to hear the Queen's Speech.

Then the Prime Minister and the Leader of the Opposition lead the M.P.s to the bar of the House of Lords, where they stand, and with apparent humility listen to the speech, which is read by the queen as though she were telling Parliament what she wished to be done. In reality the whole speech expresses the policy of the governing party in Parliament, and has been written by the Prime Minister,

57 Queen Elizabeth II giving Maundy money on the Thursday before Easter. She and Prince Philip are just leaving Westminster Abbey after giving each of a number of poor old people a purse containing £4·25. In the Middle Ages it was the custom for the king to wash the feet of as many poor men as he was years old, and then give them meat, money and clothes. Later special Maundy pennies were distributed instead

58 Queen Elizabeth II, accompanied by her husband, the Duke of Edinburgh, launches the navy's destroyer, H.M.S. *Sheffield*

who now stands humbly listening as though he were receiving the queen's instructions. Even the Lords sitting in state before the queen may owe their rank to the present or to a previous Prime Minister.

All the many titles and honours awarded to citizens and to foreigners are bestowed officially by the queen, but the recipients are chosen by the Prime Minister. The decorations are given mainly in the New Year and the Queen's Birthday Honours Lists. They may be awarded for services to industry, to the arts, to sport, to charities, and to local and national government public services. The monarchy thus becomes a political instrument in the service of the nation working through the government of the day.

The queen's life is largely made up of the observance of activities and customs dating far back in the country's history: she attends Westminster Abbey on Maundy Thursday and gives specially minted money to a number of poor men and women; she leads the splendid procession of Knights at the ceremony of the Garter at Windsor; she attends the race course at Ascot, and takes a ceremonial drive along the course, and she attends innumerable functions, and interviews many important foreign visitors.

The queen has an official birthday in May or June, and then the Trooping of the Colour takes place. Regiments of the Household troops, the Life Guards and the Horse Guards, wearing their ceremonial scarlet uniforms, march past the queen at alternating slow and normal marching pace to the sound of military bands, in a manner recalling the days when the regimental colours were carried into battle, and formed the rallying point in the fighting.

The Duke of Edinburgh, the queen's consort, takes a special interest in industry, and has instituted a number of awards for achievement in industry and technology.

12 The Power and Functions of the Monarchy Today, and its Future

No political rules can be laid down about the Crown. But on the whole it is wise in human affairs and in the government of men, to separate pomp from power.

WINSTON CHURCHILL in Ottawa, 1952.

Advice and Well-considered Inaction

The powers of the British monarch have gradually been whittled away over the course of the last three centuries, and although on a few occasions an unusual set of circumstances has given the monarch the opportunity to exercise a decisive choice, the statement made by Bagehot in 1867 remains true today – the monarch can advise, warn and encourage. Bagehot added – 'Probably in most cases the greatest wisdom of a constitutional king would show itself in well-considered inaction.' A monarch who has reigned for many years, however, may be able to give excellent advice, for his experience will in some respects be wider than that of any of his Prime Ministers. The monarch sees the papers and discusses the policy of all his Prime Ministers, of all parties; he has thus seen papers of an outgoing government of which the incoming Prime Minister will have no knowledge. As Mr Asquith wrote, 'It is not, however, the Sovereign's function to act as arbiter or mediator between rival parties and policies, still less to take advice from the leaders on both sides, with a view to forming a conclusion of his own.'

There are, of course, many things that are done in the name of the queen, things in fact which the monarch alone can do. In theory nobody but the sovereign can dismiss or appoint a Prime Minister, or summon, prorogue or dissolve Parliament. No Bill can become law without the royal assent. It is the sovereign who grants honours and creates peers of the realm. In practice, however, these things are done only on the advice of the Prime Minister, and it is most unlikely today that the sovereign would refuse to take the advice of the Prime Minister on these matters.

The Sovereign and the Choice of Prime Minister

One of the rights of the sovereign had long been that of choosing the next Prime Minister. In practice, by the beginning of the nineteenth century, there was usually little choice, and the only possible Prime Minister was the man who could command a majority in the House of Commons. In 1963, however, when Mr Macmillan had resigned, there were three leading Conservatives who might have been able to form a government, and the queen could have exercised a choice. After his resignation, Mr Macmillan could not constitutionally offer any responsible advice, but the queen then asked him to advise her, and he suggested, not any of the three main contenders, but Lord Home. The queen need not have accepted his suggestion, but without taking the opinion of any other leading Conservatives, she summoned Lord Home. She might well herself have preferred Lord Home, but she certainly seemed to have created a precedent by allowing the retiring Prime Minister to choose his successor. Two years later the Conservative Party followed the example of the other two main parties, and adopted the practice of electing a leader, whether they were in Office or in Opposition. The sovereign therefore no longer has any choice at all in the appointment of the Prime Minister.

There are still one or two hypothetical situations in which the sovereign might feel it a duty to refuse to accept the Prime Minister's advice, or give his assent to a Bill until a general election had been held, and confirmed the Prime Minister's advice. Such a situation might arise if a Parliament passed a Bill prolonging its own life for an indefinite period. The sovereign might maintain that the signing of such a Bill would not be consistent with the Coronation Oath to govern according to the 'laws and customs' of the realm. In such a use of the veto, the sovereign might be the preserver of the constitution and the liberties of the people.

The Influence of the Sovereign

Although normally the sovereign has now little direct power, she has great influence. As *Britain: An Official Handbook* says, 'The Queen is the personification of the State. In Law she is the head of the executive, an integral part of the legislature, the head of the judiciary in England and Wales, Northern Ireland

60 A Royal Family Group. Members of the Royal Family—the Queen, Prince Philip, Princess Anne and Prince Andrew visiting the Horse Trials at Badminton, using a Landrover as a grandstand

and Scotland, the Commander-in-Chief of all the Armed forces of the Crown and the temporal head of the established Church of England.'

The monarchy is thus a mainly conservative force, helping to ensure stability, but as Norman St John-Stevas says, this very fundamental stability enables the country to absorb more radical changes in its political and social structure than would otherwise be possible without real risk or disorder. It moderates the bitterness of party strife, he says, by providing a focus of loyalty which is common to all parties in the State. Or, as Malcolm Muggeridge said, monarchy is a bridge between what is fluctuating and what is everlasting in human affairs.

As the personification of the State, the monarch has tremendous prestige, and many people hold the mistaken belief that the queen still retains, and probably exercises the power to make many policy decisions for herself. In a recent public opinion survey, 40 per cent thought 'the Queen should be able to change what Parliament decides, if she disagrees with it.'

It is less as a personification of the State than as the epitome of the family, the representatives of the nation, and the symbol of what the ordinary people feel to be the essence of the English way of life, that royalty today exercises its greatest influence. As Mr Enoch Powell said, 'The Monarchy is emotional, symbolical, totemistic and mystical.' But there is quite another side to the royal family. Behind the pageantry and protocol, the royal family is much like most families. Clive Irving says, 'How grateful we should be, for this Royal Family being the way it is. Because they are, above all, very ordinary people – none of them gifted in a way which makes the ardour of the royal routine a great sacrifice of thwarted talents, none of them is mad or otherwise eccentric, none of them, as far as we know, indulges the rapacious appetites which enlivened the courts of their forebears, and none falls short of the demands of a role in life which would send most of us to the limits of despair were it ours.' But if, as Gilbert said, 'they do nothing in particular, they do it very well.'

The unenviable Position of the Monarch
The position of the monarch is indeed in many respects an unenviable one. It has always been beset by dangers and difficulties. Queen Elizabeth I said, 'To be a king and wear a crown is more glorious to them that see it than it is a pleasure to them that bear it.'

> For God's sake, let us sit upon the ground
> And tell sad stories of the death of kings

said Shakespeare's Richard II;

> How some have been deposed; some slain in war;
> Some haunted by the ghosts they have deposed:
> Some poison'd by their wives; some sleeping kill'd;

All murder'd: for within the hollow crown
That rounds the mortal temples of a king
Keeps Death his court and there the antic sits,
Scoffing his state and grinning at his pomp,
Allowing him a breath, a little scene,
To monarchize, be fear'd and kill with looks,
Infusing him with self and vain conceit
As if this flesh which walls about our life
Were brass impregnable, and humour'd thus
Comes at the last and with a little pin
Bores through his castle wall, and farewell king!
. . .

The trials of sovereigns today are different. As Harold Nicolson says, 'he learns that it is his duty to obey the government and to suffer fools with patience; he learns how to endure ceremony without manifesting overt signs of boredom; he learns how to be discreet in utterance and pleasing in appearance; he learns dignity; he learns humility under grandeur. Realising that for the vast majority of his subjects he represents the enhancement and idealisation of the national character, his domestic life will be an example of constancy, austerity and self-denial . . . he will be aware that the slightest indiscretion, the momentary display of petulance or exhaustion, will be observed, reported and magnified. He will know that he is condemned under the glare of arc-lights, to a life-sentence of hard labour. . . . In fact, he must surrender his personality to the exigencies of his task. He is bound in the process to become something of an automaton. I accord him my reverence and compassion.'

Some opponents of monarchy make it one of their main arguments that no person should be condemned to live such an unnatural life. A hundred years ago, when there were still vivid memories of the reprobate spendthrift Georges, M. Davidson wrote – 'It is not that kings and queens are worse naturally than other men and women. It is the institution that corrupts and degrades them below the level of their fellows. Let us demand the abolition of kingship in the interest of kings as well as in the interest of those whom they misgovern. No community has a right to place man or woman in a position where the temptations to vice are such as to render virtue next to impossible.' Today it is not virtue which is next to impossible for the sovereign, but spontaneity, a natural life, and, dare one suggest it, an opportunity to depart from the narrow path of virtue.

Republicanism Today
There is no strong movement today in favour of republicanism, as there was in 1870, but there are still some who object to the whole idea of monarchy, and others who, while accepting the principle, criticise certain aspects of its present form.

The main argument of the former group is that in a democratic society, where merit and not privilege or birth is considered to be the criterion for office, the monarchy is essentially non-democratic. H. G. Wells was a life-long republican, and in 1944 he wrote, 'I have always regarded and written of monarchy as a profoundly corrupting influence upon our national life, imposing an intricate snobbishness on our dominant classes, upon our religious, educational, military, naval and combatant services generally, burking the promotion of capable men and reserving power in the community entirely for the priveleged supporters of our Hanoverian Monarchy.' Leonard Woolf described monarchy as a debilitating survival from an irrational past, deliberately maintained in the interests of privilege, so perpetuating the class system.

But most men are not rational – they are largely moved by unconscious feelings and attitudes, they readily follow a leader who through the magic of personality or of exalted position, can win their support. It is suggested that it is far better that such allegiance should be attached to a hereditary monarch whose conduct is controlled by constitutional custom, than that it should be free to support men such as Hitler.

Clive Irving suggests that the best case for the monarchy is apparent simply by considering the alternative – 'Its value becomes persuasive for me,' he says 'in the

61 A Presidential election campaign in the U.S.A.

way that it acts as a buffer between the armed forces and the political machine. We have, fortunately, no tradition in Britain of generals seeking to become head of State.'

An elective monarchy, or presidency lacks both the continuity and the impartiality of a hereditary constitutional monarchy. Frequent elections are unsettling and wasteful of time and resources, but the main disadvantage of an elective head of state is that he lacks that deep psychological and emotional appeal which kings and queens seem to have for the mass of the people.

A number of public opinion surveys were made in the 1960s on the attitude of the British people to the monarchy. These surveys covered samples representative of all age groups and social classes. When asked if they favoured royalty as a method of government, 60 per cent were entirely favourable, 9 per cent largely favourable, but had some criticism, 7 per cent had mixed feelings, 3 per cent were largely unfavourable, 10 per cent entirely unfavourable, and 11 per cent uninterested. When asked if they would prefer monarchy to a republic, the first group rose to 68 per cent and the entirely unfavourable increased to 13 per cent. More women (67 per cent) were favourable than men (53 per cent), and more elderly people (73 per cent in the over 65s) than young (54 per cent in the 16 to 24 age group). Rather more of the upper and middle class (67 per cent) were favourable than lower middle class (59 per cent); skilled working class (58 per cent) and unskilled working class (60 per cent). Sympathisers with the Conservative Party were more favourable (75 per cent) than Labour Party supporters (50 per cent).

There were similar but more pronounced differences in reaction to the idea of a republic. Twice as many men (18 per cent) as women were entirely favourable. There were four times as many in the 16–24 age group (20 per cent) as in the over 65s. Only 6 per cent of upper and middle class were favourable compared with 16 per cent skilled working class; 20 per cent of Labour Party sympathisers were entirely favourable, only 6 per cent of Conservatives.

The Labour Party had long been against monarchy and it was feared that when it first gained office the monarchy and the House of Lords and much of the power of the Establishment would be swept away. Nothing of the sort. The Labour ministers were no revolutionaries, but good Britishers, who were glad to follow the traditions of their country. Wearing the 'blue gold-braided tail coats and white knee breeches with sword', they enjoyed being received by the king, who was very relieved, and very affable. The Establishment soon effectively absorbed nearly all the outsiders.

It would appear therefore that there is little likelihood of the British monarchy coming to an end in the foreseeable future. There is no large or influential group with more than a small fraction of its members in favour of a republic. The age group with the largest section of republican sympathisers is the youngest, and as people grow older they tend to become more conventional and conservative, so unless there is a startling change, the total number of republicans will not increase at all rapidly. In fact, if the British monarchy shows the adaptability which it has shown in the past, it may become more democratic, less class conscious, less Establishment orientated, and so cut the ground from under its critics, and diminish the amount of republican sympathy.

The Need for Monarchy

In an ideal world, where all men were swayed only by reason, and where government was always controlled by men who sought only the public good, a monarch would be unnecessary, but we have not reached that stage, and a stabilising factor is needed, and perhaps monarchy can most adequately perform that function. As Christopher Owen said, 'We need the Monarchy, as surely as a ship needs an anchor. It is the Crown which provides unity and continuity to Britain and the Commonwealth;' or, as Sir Winston Churchill told the House of Commons: 'Above the ebb and flow of party strife, the rise and fall of ministries, and individuals, the changes of public opinion or public fortune, the British Monarchy presides, ancient, calm and supreme within its function, over all the treasures that

62 Ramsay MacDonald joins the Establishment

have been saved from the past and all the glories we write in the annals of our country.'

But the monarchy is not perfect. 'True criticism of the Monarchy today,' wrote Kingsley Martin, 'is not in any way personal; nor is it constitutional. . . . In the mid-twentieth century it [the monarchy] has taken the wrong turning. The Establishment damages it by glorifying it, thus seeking to disguise the power that private persons still exercise over the nation's affairs. The Monarchy could still be respected and indeed loved, as hereditary presidency of the nation and Commonwealth. But if it maintains itself as head of a social class and a vanishing economic order it can only be a symbol of the past, and not become part of the new England that waits to be born.'

Further Reading

FURTHER READING

Blood Royal, Iain Moncreiffe and Don Pottinger (Nelson).

The Divine Right of Kings, John Neville Figgis (Harper Torchbooks, Harper & Row).

The Monarchy and its Future, Edited by J. Murray-Brown (Allen & Unwin).

Kings and Queens of England and Great Britain, E. R. Delderfield (David & Charles).

Richard III, P. M. Kendall (Allen & Unwin).

Monarchy, Harold Nicolson (Weidenfeld & Nicolson).

The Crown and The Establishment, Kingsley Martin (Hutchinson).

Long to Reign over Us, L. M. Harris (William Kimber).

The Queen Reigns: She does not Rule, F. W. G. Benemy (Harrap).

The English Constitution, W. Bagehot.

Hanover to Windsor, Roger Tulford (Batsford).

The British Constitution, Sir Ivor Jennings (Cambridge University Press).

The Stuarts, J. P. Kenyon (Batsford).

How the Queen Reigns, Dorothy Laird (Hodder & Stoughton).

The Tudors, Christopher Morris (Batsford).

King George V: His Life and Reign, Sir Harold Nicolson (Constable).

The First Four Georges, J. H. Plumb (Batsford).

Tradition and Custom in Modern Britain, L. G. Pine (Ronald Whiting and Wheaton).

Index

The numbers in **bold type** refer to the pages on which illustrations appear.